THE
RHYTHMIC
STRUCTURE
OF
MUSIC

Grosvenor W. Cooper and Leonard B. Meyer

THE
RHYTHMIC
STRUCTURE
OF
MUSIC

ISBN: 0-226-11521-6 (clothbound); 0-226-11522-4 (paperbound)
Library of Congress Catalog Card Number: 60-14068

THE UNIVERSITY OF CHICAGO PRESS, CHICAGO 60637
The University of Chicago Press, Ltd., London

PREFACE

Every musician, whether composer, performer, or theorist will agree that "In the beginning was rhythm." For the shaping power of rhythm and, more broadly speaking, of the temporal organization of music, is a *sine qua non* of the art. An understanding of rhythm is important for performer as well as composer, for historian as well as music theorist. Yet the study of this aspect of music has been almost totally neglected in the formal training of musicians since the Renaissance. There are many textbooks on harmony and counterpoint but none on rhythm. Although theorists have frequently written about the temporal organization of music, their concern has generally been with meter and phrase structure rather than with rhythm. Every music school requires students to take courses in harmony and counterpoint, but few give more than passing notice to the rhythmic structure of music.

A book dealing with rhythm must therefore perform two functions at once. It must, on the one hand, organize and develop a conceptual framework—a theory of rhythmic structure. And it must, on the other hand, present through discussion, example, and precept, analytical methods and compositional procedures.

This book does not presume to answer all questions in the field of rhythm. Nor does it pretend to cover all possible rhythmic problems. It is a first book on the subject, a text intended for students not too advanced in theoretical studies but already familiar with harmony and counterpoint. It is also a beginning in the sense that it will, we hope, lead to further study of rhythm and better, more comprehensive texts.

Since there are at present very few courses in rhythm, this book is designed to be used in conjunction with courses in harmony or counterpoint, courses in interpretation, and courses in analysis. It has been successfully used in these ways at the University of Chicago. We hope that, as a result of its existence, courses dealing with rhythm will begin to be offered as part of the music curriculum.

We are well aware of the fact that some readers will take exception either to the general conceptual framework advanced here or to particular analyses. With regard to the former, we can but hope that dissenting voices will provoke a fruitful discussion on a subject which has, by seemingly common consent, been neglected by music theorists. With regard to the latter, we can but plead fallibility and emphasize that what is crucial in the present undertaking is the method and general viewpoint rather than their exemplifications in any particular analysis.

This book is the result of many fruitful, and some fruitless, discussions—and sometimes arguments—which we have had both with our colleagues and with our students. The debt which we owe to them is freely acknowledged. In particular we wish to thank Mrs. Jeanne Bamberger, whose many helpful suggestions and cogent criticism have found their way into this book.

CONTENTS

I *Definitions and Principles 1*

      Architectonic Levels 2

      Pulse *3*

      Meter *4*

      Rhythm *6*

      Accent *7*

      Stress *8*

      Grouping *8*

II *Rhythms on Lower Architectonic Levels 12*

      Trochee and Iamb in Duple Meter *12*

      Articulation and Structure *17*

      Amphibrach, Anapest, and Dactyl in Duple Meter *18*

      Dactyl, Anapest, and Amphibrach in Triple Meter *23*

      The Character of Particular Rhythms *26*

      Iamb and Trochee in Triple Meter *29*

      Rhythmic Ambiguity *32*

      The Influence of Rhythm on Melodic Motion *36*

      Recapitulation and Illustration *37*

      Exercises *57*

III *More Complex Rhythmic Structures 60*

      Theoretical Considerations *61*

      The Coherence of Higher-Level Rhythms *62*

Groupings on Higher Levels   *68*
Analysis of a Whole Section   *83*
Exercises   *87*

IV   *Rhythm and Meter*   *88*

Meter and the Bar Line   *88*
Non-congruence   *89*
The Influence of Stress upon Meter   *98*
Syncopations, Suspensions, and Ties   *99*
Metric Crossing   *106*
Exercises   *115*

V   *Rhythm, Mobility, and Tension*   *117*

Rhythm and Mobility   *117*
Rhythm and Tension   *125*
An Extended Anacrusis   *129*
An Accented Rest   *137*
Summary Example   *140*
Exercises   *142*

VI   *Rhythm, Continuity, and Form*   *144*

Rhythm, Form, and Morphological Lengths   *144*
Continuity and Form   *147*
Themes, Non-themes, and Continuity   *153*
Rhythm and Texture   *160*
Exercises   *167*

VII   *Rhythmic Development*   *168*

Ambiguous Rhythm   *168*
Rhythmic Vagueness   *171*
Rhythmic Transformation   *174*
Anacrustic Development   *177*
Exercises   *182*

VIII *Extended Examples 183*

Chopin, Prelude in E-flat, Op. 24   *185*

Beethoven, Symphony No. 8, First Movement   *188*

List of Symbols 204

Index 205

Index of Music 208

I DEFINITIONS AND PRINCIPLES

To study rhythm is to study all of music. Rhythm both organizes, and is itself organized by, all the elements which create and shape musical processes.

Just as a melody is more than simply a series of pitches, so rhythm is more than a mere sequence of durational proportions. To experience rhythm is to group separate sounds into structured patterns. Such grouping is the result of the interaction among the various aspects of the materials of music: pitch, intensity, timbre, texture, and harmony—as well as duration.

It is the intimate and intricate interaction of temporal organization with all the other shaping forces of music which makes the study of rhythm both a rewarding task and, at times, a difficult and perplexing one. The task is rewarding not only because the subject is itself intrinsically interesting but also because, by adding a new dimension to our understanding of related fields such as melody, harmony, counterpoint, and orchestration, it makes possible a more precise and penetrating analysis of those processes.

The study of rhythm is rewarding in a practical way as well. An understanding of rhythm is as important to the performer as it is to the composer and to the theorist. Indeed, as will be apparent throughout this book, a considerable part of what is usually called "interpretation" depends upon the performer's sensitivity to and awareness of rhythmic structure.

Because the complex and delicate interaction among the elements of music precludes the use of easy "rules of thumb" and pat, simplistic answers, the analysis of rhythm tends to be complicated and, at times, uncertain. These difficulties are in part responsible for the neglect which the field of rhythm has suffered in recent writings on music theory.

In part, however, the development of a fruitful approach to the study of rhythm has been hampered by a failure to distinguish clearly among the several aspects of temporal organization itself. The resulting confusion has created a correlative ambiguity of terminology. Since clear distinctions and unequivocal terminology are necessary if the analysis of the rhythmic structure of music is to move beyond its present moribund state, our first task must be one of definition.

Some of the distinctions and definitions presented in what follows may seem un-usual or contrary to current use. We ask the reader to bear with us, trusting that he will find that the insights which the distinctions ultimately yield will justify the inconvenience of novelty.

ARCHITECTONIC LEVELS

Most of the music with which we shall be concerned is architectonic in its organization. That is, just as letters are combined into words, words into sen-tences, sentences into paragraphs, and so on, so in music individual tones be-come grouped into motives, motives into phrases, phrases into periods, etc. This is a familiar concept in the analysis of harmonic and melodic structure. It is equally important in the analysis of rhythm and meter.

As a piece of music unfolds, its rhythmic structure is perceived not as a series of discrete independent units strung together in a mechanical, additive way like beads, but as an organic process in which smaller rhythmic motives, while possessing a shape and structure of their own, also function as integral parts of a larger rhythmic organization. In Example 53a (p. 42), for instance, the motive of the first measure forms a small, separate rhythmic group. When this motive is repeated in the second measure, the motive and its repetition are perceived as constituting a more extended rhythmic pattern. They form a rhythm on a higher architectonic level.

The lowest level on which a complete rhythmic group is realized—upon which a strong beat and one or more weak beats are grouped together—will be called the *primary rhythmic level*. As is often the case, the rhythm of the primary level in Example 53a is itself made up of smaller note values which form a subsidiary, partial rhythmic motive. Such partial patterns create what will be called *inferior rhythmic levels* or, where there is only one such level, the *subprimary level*. When groups on the primary rhythmic level are themselves organized into longer, compound patterns, *superior rhythmic levels* are created.

In the analyses given in this book the schematization of the primary level will be indicated by an arabic "1." Superior levels, in order of increasing length, will be labeled "2," "3," etc. Inferior rhythmic levels, in order of decreasing length, will be indicated by small roman numerals: "i," "ii," etc. (see Examples 23 and 50, pp. 23, 40).

Metric structure is similarly architectonic. For instance, a $\frac{3}{4}$ meter differs from a $\frac{6}{8}$ meter in that the former is made up of three units of a lower level $\frac{2}{8}$ meter, while the latter is made up of two units of a lower level $\frac{3}{8}$ meter. And either a $\frac{3}{4}$ or a $\frac{6}{8}$ meter may itself be combined with metric units on the same level to form more extensive, higher-level meters. Thus in Example 53a the meter of the primary level—the level on which beats are felt and counted—is in threes. The inferior metric level is organized in twos ($\frac{2}{8}$) and the superior metric level is also duple—that is, $2 \times \frac{3}{4}$.

Three basic modes of temporal organization can be differentiated. They are pulse, meter, and rhythm. Tempo, though it qualifies and modifies these, is not itself a mode of organization. Thus a rhythm or theme will be recognizably the same whether played faster or slower. And while changes in tempo will alter the character of the music and perhaps influence our impression of what the basic beat is (since the beat tends to be perceived as being moderate in speed), tempo is not a relationship. It is not an organizing force.[1]

PULSE

A pulse is one of a series of regularly recurring, precisely equivalent stimuli. Like the ticks of a metronome or a watch, pulses mark off equal units in the temporal continuum. Though generally established and supported by objective stimuli (sounds), the sense of pulse may exist subjectively. A sense of regular pulses, once established, tends to be continued in the mind and musculature of the listener, even though the sound has stopped. For instance, objective pulses may cease or may fail for a time to coincide with the previously established pulse series. When this occurs, the human need for the security of an actual stimulus or for simplicity of response generally makes such passages seem to point toward the re-establishment of objective pulses or to a return to pulse coincidence.

All pulses in a series are by definition exactly alike. However, preferring clear and definite patterns to such an unorganized and potentially infinite series, the human mind tends to impose some sort of organization upon such equal pulses.[2] As we listen to the ticks of a clock or the clicks of a railroad car passing over the tracks, we tend to arrange the equal pulses into intelligible units of finite duration or into even more obviously structured groups. Thus, although pulse can theoretically exist without either meter or rhythm, the nature of the human mind is such that this is a rare occurrence in music.

While pulse is seldom heard in a pure state (as a series of undifferentiated stimuli), this does not mean that it is not an important aspect of musical ex-

[1] It is important to recognize that tempo is a psychological fact as well as a physical one. Thus eighth-notes in two pieces of music may move at the same absolute speed, but one of the pieces may seem faster than the other. This is possible because the psychological tempo, which we shall call "pace," depends upon how time is filled—upon how many patterns arise in a given span of time. See, for instance, the increase in pace which takes place at measure 48 in the second movement of Mozart's Piano Concerto in D Minor (K. 466).

[2] That the mind tends to impose patterns upon even a random series of stimuli has been clearly demonstrated by experiments. See John Cohen, "Subjective Probability," *Scientific American*, XCCVII, No. 5 (November, 1957), 136.

perience. Not only is pulse necessary for the existence of meter, but it generally, though not always, underlies and reinforces rhythmic experience.

METER

Meter is the measurement of the number of pulses between more or less regularly recurring accents.[3] Therefore, in order for meter to exist, some of the pulses in a series must be accented—marked for consciousness—relative to others.[4] When pulses are thus counted within a metric context, they are referred to as *beats*. Beats which are accented are called "strong"; those which are unaccented are called "weak."

While there can be no meter without an underlying pulse to establish the units of measurement, there can, as we shall see, be meter without any clearly definable rhythm (see pp. 7–8). Conversely, there can be rhythm without meter—as in the "free" rhythm of some Oriental and folk music and in what has been called the "measured rhythm" of Gregorian chant.[5]

Although meter tends to be regular, irregularities may occur without destroying the sense of metric organization.[6] Usually this is because such irregularities are temporary. Often too, what is irregular on one architectonic level becomes regular on a higher (or lower) one. Thus if a unit of three quarter-notes is followed by a unit of two and the tempo is quite fast, the mind, tending to perceive a pattern in the simplest, most regular way possible, will organize the pattern into a composite group of five quarter-notes, as in Act III, scene 2 (measures 31 ff.) of Wagner's *Tristan und Isolde*. This is also the case with the hemiole rhythm in which the opposition of three groups of two played against two groups of three $\left(\begin{smallmatrix} 2+2+2 \\ 3+3 \end{smallmatrix}\right)$ is resolved after six beats. Indeed, one might state as a general law that the dominant or primary meter will tend to organize itself—be perceived—on the lowest architectonic level on which it exhibits regularity.

As noted above, meter, like other aspects of musical organization, is architectonic in nature. That is, since the beats which measure the meter designated in the time signature may themselves be divided into equal units or compounded

[3] Although theorists, both Renaissance and modern, have referred to the measurement of regularly recurring accents as "rhythm," it is not so by our definition. And it would seem that only confusion has resulted from calling those aspects of temporal organization which measure, "rhythmic." They are metric.

[4] For further discussion of "accent," see pp. 11 ff.

[5] See Willi Apel, *Harvard Dictionary of Music* (Cambridge, Mass.: Harvard University Press, 1945), p. 640.

[6] Often such irregularities are not apparent in the time signature of the music. This is the case with the hemiole "rhythm," for instance. Conversely, meter may at times be more regular than its notation would lead us to expect. For such an example, see Leonard B. Meyer, *Emotion and Meaning in Music* (Chicago: University of Chicago Press, 1956), pp. 119–21.

into larger metric units, some of which will be accented relative to others, it follows that most compositions present a hierarchy of metric organizations. For instance, the units of a $\frac{2}{4}$ meter might be divided or compounded as in Example 1. Needless to say, other combinations are possible on all architectonic levels.

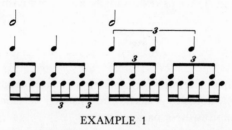

EXAMPLE 1

We are inclined to think of there being only one metric organization, the one designated in the time signature and measured by the bar lines. This is because tonal harmony and homophony, with their emphasis upon vertical coincidence, and dance music, with its basic motor patterns, have for the past two hundred years made for the dominance of what we have called the "primary metric level." Until recently this primary level has dominated metric experience. Changes on other metric levels which can be and are referred to the regularity of the primary level are treated with an almost casual freedom.

But this has not always been the case. In the polyphonic music of the later Middle Ages and the Renaissance the relationships of the several metric levels both within each voice and between voices was a very important facet of style. The organization of these metric levels was recognized by the theorists of the time and was specified by the time signatures of the period. Such terms as "tempus," "prolatio," "perfectus," and so forth indicated the organization on particular metric levels.

Of course some time signatures do indicate the organization of inferior metric levels. Thus $\frac{3}{4}$ implies—but only implies—that the subsidiary metric organization is to be in twos. One can easily move from this organization in twos, ♫ ♫ ♫ , to the one in threes, ♪♪♪ ♪♪♪ ♪♪♪ , as Schubert, for instance, was so fond of doing. There are only a few instances in the literature of music since 1600 in which the composer has specified what the metric organization of higher architectonic levels is to be. The example which comes to mind most readily occurs in the Scherzo (measures 180–240) of Beethoven's Symphony No. 9, where the composer indicates that the higher rhythmic organization is to be in threes or in fours by writing "ritmo di tre battute" or "ritmo di quattro battute" (see Example 95, p. 80).

RHYTHM

Rhythm may be defined as the way in which one or more unaccented beats are grouped in relation to an accented one. The five basic rhythmic groupings may be differentiated by terms traditionally associated with prosody:

<blockquote>
a. iamb ∪ —
b. anapest ∪ ∪ —
c. trochee — ∪
d. dactyl — ∪ ∪
e. amphibrach ∪ — ∪
</blockquote>

Since, as noted above, rhythmic organization is architectonic, more extensive rhythmic structures—phrases, periods, etc.—as well as shorter, more obviously rhythmic motives exhibit these basic patterns.

Rhythm is independent of meter in two separate senses. First, rhythm can exist without there being a regular meter, as it does in the case of Gregorian chant or recitativo secco. That is, unaccented notes may be grouped in relation to an accented one without there being regularly recurring accents measuring metric units of equal duration. Indeed, rhythm is at least theoretically independent of pulse. Second, and more important for our purposes, rhythm is independent of meter in the sense that any one of the rhythmic groupings given above can occur in any type of metric organization. For instance, an iambic grouping can occur in duple or triple meter. In other words, rhythm can vary within a given metric organization, as the examples in the following chapters amply illustrate.

Though rhythm may vary independently of meter, this does not mean that rhythm is not influenced by the metric organization and, conversely, that meter is not in a very important sense dependent upon rhythm. As we shall see, some rhythmic groupings are more difficult to realize in a given meter than others. On the other hand, precisely because rhythmic accents generally coincide with metric ones, it should be emphasized that the bar lines, which serve to mark off metric units, do not indicate what the rhythmic organization is. Rhythmic groups are not respecters of bar lines. They cross them more often than not; and one of the first things that the reader must learn is that the bar line will tell him little about rhythmic grouping.

Since a rhythmic group can be apprehended only when its elements are distinguished from one another, rhythm, as defined above, always involves an interrelationship between a single, accented (strong) beat and either one or two unaccented (weak) beats. Hence neither a series of undifferentiated strong beats (− −, etc.), the so-called spondee foot, nor a series of undifferentiated weak beats (∪∪, etc.), the pyrrhic foot, can be true rhythms. They are incomplete rhythms (see pp. 85 ff.). Other possible combinations of strong and weak beats, such as ♫ ♩ ♪ (∪ ∪ − ∪) or ♩ ♪♩ (− ∪ −), will be analyzed as combinations of the basic groups given above, and , rather than as separate, independent patterns. In addition to limiting the number of classifiable patterns, this procedure has the advantage of employing a single method for analyzing group formation on all architectonic levels.

The use of poetic feet to analyze rhythmic patterns is somewhat unusual.[7] Rhythmic groupings have generally been treated as if they were metric units. However, since these groups can be found in various different meters they are not themselves the same as meters. An account of the theoretical basis for the viewpoint advanced here is beyond the scope of this book.[8] We can but ask the reader, at least provisionally, to accept this viewpoint and hope that he will find it justified by the understanding which it yields.

ACCENT

Though the concept of accent is obviously of central importance in the theory and analysis of rhythm, an ultimate definition in terms of psychological causes does not seem possible with our present knowledge. That is, one cannot at present state unequivocally what makes one tone seem accented and another not. For while such factors as duration, intensity, melodic contour, regularity, and so forth obviously play a part in creating an impression of accent, none of them appears to be an invariable and necessary concomitant of accent.[9] Accents may occur on short notes as well as long, on soft notes as well as loud, on lower notes as well as higher ones, and irregularly as well as regularly. In short, since accent appears to be a product of a number of variables whose interaction is not precisely known, it must for our purposes remain a basic, axiomatic concept which is understandable as an experience but undefined in terms of causes.

However, while we cannot stipulate precisely what makes a tone seem accented, we can define accent in terms of its operation within the musical context and point out many of its characteristics. In order for a tone to appear accented it must be set off from other tones of the series in some way. If all notes are alike, there will be no accents. At the same time, however, the accented tone must be similar and near enough to other tones of the series that it can be related to these—that it does not become an isolated sound. In other words, accent is a

---

[7] As Apel (*op. cit.*, p. 639) points out, "It would be a hopeless task to search for a definition of rhythm which would prove acceptable even to a small minority of musicians and writers on music."

[8] See Meyer, *op. cit.*, pp. 83–93 and 102 ff.; and James I. Mursell, *The Psychology of Music* (New York: W. W. Norton, 1937), chaps. iv and v.

[9] While accents may be distinguished according to whether they are produced by stress (dynamic), duration (agogic), or melodic change (tonic), their function in organizing rhythmic groups does not depend upon their origin and we have therefore decided to treat them as a single aspect of rhythmic experience. See Apel, *op. cit.*, p. 6.

relational concept. There can be accents only if there are unaccents (weak beats) and vice versa. In this sense there is no such thing as a series of accents or a series of weak beats. If all stimuli are alike, there is only a series of pulses.

An accent, then, is a stimulus (in a series of stimuli) which is *marked for consciousness* in some way. It is set off from other stimuli because of differences in duration, intensity, pitch, timbre, etc. But in a sense so are the unaccented beats thus distinguished. The difference between accented and unaccented beats lies in the fact that the accented beat is the focal point, the nucleus of the rhythm, around which the unaccented beats are grouped and in relation to which they are heard. This is clear when it is noticed that a rhythmic group may have several unaccented beats, which may precede or follow the accent (or both), but a rhythmic group may have but one accent on any given architectonic level. Furthermore, as we shall see presently, an unaccented beat may belong to more than one rhythmic group, while an accent, because it is the focal point about which weak beats are arranged, generally belongs to only one rhythmic group.

Finally, accented beats differ from unaccented ones in that their placement in the series of beats tends to be fixed and stable. Specifically, in order to obtain the desired impression of grouping, the performer often slightly displaces unaccented beats in the temporal continuum so that they are closer in time to the accents with which they are to be grouped than if he had played them with rigid precision. (The rubato style of playing would seem to be an instance of such displacement.) But accented beats seem never to be so displaced.

STRESS

Accent must not be confused with stress. The term "stress," as used in this book, means the dynamic intensification of a beat, whether accented or unaccented. Thus a stress, no matter how forceful, placed on a weak beat will not make that beat accented.

While stress does not change the function of beats, it may and often does change the grouping of the beats—the rhythm. In general it appears that stress, whether on a weak or strong beat, tends to mark the beginning of a group. Thus, as we shall see, a normally end-accented (iamb or anapest) temporal organization may be made beginning-accented (trochee or dactyl) by placing a stress on the accent (see Examples 19 and 20, pp. 20, 21), while a normally beginning-accented group may be converted into an end-accented one by placing a stress upon a weak beat (see Example 21, pp. 21).

GROUPING

Since this book is in fact concerned throughout with grouping—for that is what rhythm is—the following discussion of the general principles of grouping will be minimal. Its purpose, which is practical rather than theoretical, is to make the reader aware of a few of the basic concepts and procedures used in this book and thus help him to understand what follows and aid him in his own analyses.

Rhythmic grouping is a mental fact, not a physical one. There are no hard and fast rules for calculating what in any particular instance the grouping is. Sensitive, well-trained musicians may differ. Indeed, it is this that makes performance an art—that makes different phrasings and different interpretations of a piece of music possible. Furthermore, grouping may at times be purposefully ambiguous and must be thus understood rather than forced into a clear decisive pattern. In brief, the interpretation of music—and this is what analysis should be—is an art requiring experience, understanding, and sensitivity.

Grouping on all architectonic levels is a product of similarity and difference, proximity and separation of the sounds perceived by the senses and organized by the mind. If tones are in no way differentiated from one another—whether in pitch, range, instrumentation and timbre, duration, intensity, texture, or dynamics—then there can be no rhythm or grouping. For the mind will have no basis for perceiving one tone as accented and others as unaccented. There will be uniform pulses, nothing more, unless of course the grouping is completely subjective. On the other hand, if the successive stimuli are so different from one another or so separate in time or pitch that the mind cannot relate them to one another, there will be no impression of rhythm. The stimuli will then be perceived as separate, isolated tones.

In general, sounds or groups of sounds which are similar (in timbre, volume, etc.) and near to each other (in time, pitch, etc.) form strongly unified rhythmic patterns. Difference and distance between sounds or groups of sounds tend to separate rhythmic patterns. However, though *similarity* tends to create cohesion, repetition usually makes for the separation of groups. The case is somewhat different when a single pitch is repeated. For though such repetition may at first give rise to group cohesion, as it continues, change is expected. Consequently the final note or notes of the series will seem like anacruses (upbeats) and will become grouped with the new tone to which they move.

Except on the lowest architectonic level, a grouping is seldom the result of the action of all the elements of music (duration, pitch, harmony, instrumentation, etc.). Both within and between groups, some of the elements of music will tend to produce group coherence, others will tend to produce group separation. For instance, in measure 1 of Example 2 (p. 12) the grouping of beats 1 and 2 together and beats 3 and 4 together—the lowest architectonic level—is a result of the similarity and proximity of pitch, duration, and harmony. These two groups combine to form a group on the next architectonic level. This larger group is held together by temporal proximity and harmony, but it is separated into two subgroups by non-proximity of pitch and difference of timbre, since the latter element tends to change, if only slightly, with the change in pitch.

This division of function among the several elements of music in which some produce unity and others separation is one of the things which at times make it difficult to know what the dominant grouping is. In any particular case is melodic segregation marked enough to outweigh harmonic similarity and temporal proximity? Do instrumental differences dominate grouping in another case, or does harmonic similarity dominate? And so forth. Again, it is partly the fact that no hard and fast rules can be established to solve this problem of the precedence of variables that makes analysis an art rather than a science.

In this admittedly difficult problem of grouping there is, however, one fundamental set of rules for the organization of relationships within groups: Durational differences, which necessarily result in the temporal proximity of some stimuli and therefore in the separation of others, tend to produce end-accented groupings (iambs and anapests); intensity differentiation tends to produce beginning-accented groupings (trochees and dactyls); and the proper combination of durational difference with intensity difference tends to produce middle-accented groupings (amphibrachs).

Thus if we have a series of evenly spaced beats and every third one, beginning with the first, is accented, the rhythm will be dactylic:

Now if we keep intensity constant and gradually lengthen the relative duration of the accented beat, making the weak beats closer to the accent which follows them, until this temporal disposition is reached, the grouping will become end-accented, that is, anapestic:

However, if we change the temporal placement of the final tone so that it is closer to the accent which follows it, the organization will be perceived as an amphibrach grouping, that is, as middle-accented:

But even if there is durational equality, as in the first case, the grouping can be heard as end-accented. There are two reasons for this. In the first place, duration is not the only factor determining grouping; an end-accented group might easily arise if the second and third beats were closer in pitch to the beat which follows them than they were to the beat which precedes them. Or if the two final beats were separated from the first beat in tonal function and harmony—for instance, if they were on the seventh degree of the scale and moved to the tonic on the following beat—then they would be grouped with the tone to which they move. In this sense, the grouping depends upon whether tones are moving from a goal or are moving toward one. In the second place, if the mind imposes an end-accented grouping upon this durational disposition—if this is to be heard as an anapest—then the last two notes will be performed or imagined ever so slightly nearer to the accent with which they are to be grouped.[10] The notation remains the same. What changes is the interpretation of the grouping. And this change affects the placement of the beats and consequently the listener's impression of the grouping as well as the performer's expression of it. This is a crucial fact in the analysis and performance of music and one to which we shall find ourselves referring throughout this book.

[10] For experimental confirmation, see R. B. Stetson, "A Motor Theory of Rhythm and Discrete Succession," *Psychological Review*, XII (1905), 250–70, 293–350; and H. Woodrow, "A Quantitative Study of Rhythm," *Archives of Psychology*, XIV (1909), 1–66.

II RHYTHMS ON LOWER ARCHITECTONIC LEVELS

This chapter is concerned with the analysis of relatively simple rhythms on the lowest architectonic level. It is hoped that after the reader has studied it with care, performing the examples and doing the exercises, he will have learned through example as well as prescript something about (1) the nature and organization of rhythmic groups; (2) the influences of changes of pitch, duration, intensity, orchestration, and phrasing upon grouping; (3) the relationship of rhythmic groups to metric organization; (4) the differences which may exist within one type of rhythmic group; and (5) the general methods and procedures employed in the analysis of rhythm.

We shall begin with four measures of a folk song in duple meter and illustrate by a process of simple variation, in which as many factors as possible are kept constant, both the several types of rhythmic groups and the influence of changes in the elements of music on such groups. Later another folk tune in triple meter will be used to exemplify other aspects of grouping and of the relationship between rhythm and meter. Following this, in order to show how differences in the relationships of the elements of music to one another within a single type of grouping modify the effect and tendency of particular rhythms, several themes having the same basic rhythmic grouping will be analyzed. Finally, there will be a brief discussion of the influence of rhythmic organization on melodic movement.

TROCHEE AND IAMB IN DUPLE METER

The grouping of the quarter-notes in the folk tune given in Example 2 is trochaic, as is indicated by the lower brackets. The reader should note that while it is obviously necessary to discover and indicate which beats are accented and

EXAMPLE 2

which are not, this does not constitute an analysis of the rhythm. What is required is an indication of how the beats are grouped. The grouping in this example results from the proximity and similarity of the elements of sound. That is, the two quarter-notes of each trochaic group are proximate in time and identical in pitch, temporal placement, timbre, dynamics, and so forth.

Although the *dominant* organization of this tune is trochaic, it is important to realize that an end-accented, iambic grouping is not completely absent. It is the *latent* organization and helps to connect and join the series of trochees to one another. Such latent organization will be indicated, as in this example, by the use of inverted brackets.[1]

THE INFLUENCE OF DURATION

If one or more of these elements is changed, the grouping will tend to change too. For instance, if the temporal placement is altered so that the first note of the group is lengthened, making the second note closer to the note which follows it, the grouping will become iambic (Example 3). This example illustrates several

EXAMPLE 3

points important to rhythmic grouping: (1) The grouping is most clearly iambic where both temporal and melodic proximity exists between groups, as from measure 2 on. (2) The iambic character of the rhythm is emphasized if an eighth-note upbeat (either G or D) is placed (or imagined) before the first measure or when the tune is repeated with the upbeat D, as shown. This occurs because, once a rhythm becomes established, it tends, if possible, to be continued in the mind of the listener—it tends, that is, to organize later patterns in its own image. This is true even where the natural grouping would seem to be otherwise. For instance, if the reader begins Example 2 with an upbeat D, he will hear that the iambic organization seems to continue throughout the example. (3) Bar lines do not determine or delimit grouping. Only beginning-accented groups on the lowest architectonic level stay within them.

Examples 2 and 3 demonstrate the ability of temporal proximity to influence grouping. The more marked such proximity is, the more patent the grouping will be. And necessarily following from this, the more tones are separated, the greater the tendency for them to belong to different groups. For instance, if Example 2 had a temporal organization throughout such as ♫ 𝄾 ♫ 𝄾 etc., its

[1] However, when the analysis is placed *above* the music in some later examples, the upper brackets indicate the dominant organization.

trochaic grouping would be even more marked; or if Example 3 were written as  etc., its iambic organization would be even more patent.

Melodic changes can also alter grouping. If the temporal organization is kept constant (is the same as in the original tune) and the details of the melody rather than its basic melodic structure are modified in the particular way shown in Example 4, the rhythm tends to be heard as iambic. This grouping occurs be-

EXAMPLE 4

cause, given durational equality, the mind groups proximate elements together—the C with the B in measure 1, the D-sharp with the E across the bar, and so forth. Or, to put the matter the other way around, separate groups tend to arise where there is relative non-proximity—the C is separated from the G which precedes it, the D-sharp from the B, etc.

Also of importance in the articulation of this variant of the tune is the implied harmony. Each leading tone moves to and is grouped with its goal—its temporary tonic.

But even without this leading-tone effect, the grouping of the last two measures will tend to be end-accented if there is a cadence on the D in measure 2. For since this is the temporary goal of the first measure and because it resolves an appoggiatura (E), it closes out the first larger group. The B which follows must of necessity then group itself with the C. Once this pattern is established, it tends to perpetuate itself (Example 5a). However, if the B is omitted so that the C is without an anacrusis, an upbeat, the final measures can be heard as trochaic (Example 5b). They are able to form this pattern partly because each of the two-note groups belongs to the same harmony.

EXAMPLE 5

Notice that the first measure has also been changed. This illustrates the fact that pattern repetition leads to group separation. Indeed, in this case because both groups are parts of the same triad, the disjunction is marked by the repeated B.

THE INFLUENCE OF BEAT PLACEMENT

It is most important to realize that the performer's understanding of a rhythm influences his placement of the weak beats. In Example 4, for instance, the performer would unconsciously place beats 2 and 4 slightly closer to beats 3 and 1 (of the following measure) than he would in Example 2, where an apparently similar set of temporal relationships is heard as trochaic. The rhythm of the tune would be changed, even without melodic and durational alterations, were it phrased as in Example 6. Here not only would the performer indicate the grouping by a legato manner of playing, but he would also move the weak beats slightly closer to the accents which follow and he might also alter duration by cutting the length of the accented beats (as indicated by the commas), thus separating the groups. Observe that the particular effect of Example 6 is in part dependent

EXAMPLE 6

upon the fact that, particularly in the first measure, an iambic grouping is imposed upon a melodic-temporal organization which would otherwise give rise to a trochaic rhythm.

As indicated in Example 6, the performer will also articulate the desired grouping by making a slight crescendo on the upbeat. This is followed by a "piano" accent so that the next group can be performed the same way without creating an over-all crescendo. Such crescendos whether over one note or a group of notes are an important way in which groupings can be made clear. They indicate the tendency, the leading toward a goal, of a tone or a group of tones. That is, the crescendo creates an expectation that an accent will follow, and the tone bearing the crescendo is heard as leading toward, and grouping with, the expected accent.

Because the more a tone seems to be oriented toward a goal, the more it tends to function as an anacrusis, rising melodic lines, particularly conjunct ones, tend to become anacrustic. The energy and striving implicit in a rising line make each successive tone move *toward* the one which follows it, rather than *from* the one preceding it. A rising melodic line feels very much like a crescendo. Indeed, most people perceive it as such. This is shown not only by the tendency of performers to crescendo in rising passages and of composers to indicate crescendos over rising passages much more frequently than over descending ones, but also by the fact that people actually hear higher pitches as louder, even though intensity remains constant. Conversely, descending melodic lines, or those involving the repetition of one or two tones, tend generally to be heard with feminine endings (trochees or amphibrachs), each tone moving from the one before it.

THE INFLUENCE OF INSTRUMENTATION

Groupings can also be shaped, emphasized, or altered by changes in instrumentation and timbre. For instance, the original trochaic organization of the tune (Example 2) could be emphasized by playing alternate groups on different instruments in a kind of hocket technique, as in Example 7, which might be

EXAMPLE 7

played by an oboe and a violin. But even if the parts were played by two violins, the groupings would be apparent, particularly in a live performance where the difference in timbre between the violins would be accompanied by a different location of the sound source. A single instrument, too, might articulate the groupings by differences in timbre. For example, a violin might play every other group pizzicato or a trumpet might mute alternate groups.

In like manner, instrumentation and timbre might be used to organize the beats in an iambic grouping as in Examples 8 and 9. (The crosses in Example 9 represent pizzicato on a violin or muting on the trumpet.)

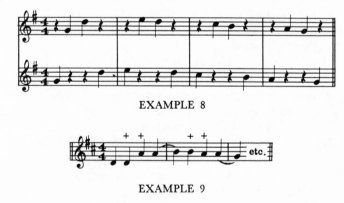

EXAMPLE 8

EXAMPLE 9

Dynamics too might be used to articulate different types of groupings. Thus if beat 1 were played forte, beats 2 and 3 piano, beats 4 and 1 forte, etc., there would be a tendency for an iambic rhythm to arise. While if beats 1 and 2 were played forte and beats 3 and 4 piano, the trochaic rhythm would be emphasized.

THE INFLUENCE OF ACCOMPANIMENT

Clearly harmony and whatever counterpoint or accompaniment figure is present, may play a decisive role in articulating grouping. Thus after a somewhat ambiguous initial measure the rhythm of Example 10 becomes iambic on the primary level once the shaping forces of harmony and voice-leading are brought into play in measure 2.

EXAMPLE 10

ARTICULATION AND STRUCTURE

Although it would be quite easy to employ all the elements of music to emphasize a particular type of grouping and achieve a kind of unmitigated iambic, trochaic, or other grouping, this is in point of fact a rare occurrence in music literature. For if all the elements are used in such a single-minded manner on the lowest architectonic level, the resulting patterns, though themselves impregnable, become so segregated from one another that there can be no higher levels of rhythmic organization. There will be no rhythms between groups within the measure and none between measures, because no elements are left to form a basis for such larger groups. This is the case in Example 11, where the groups,

EXAMPLE 11

though clearly iambic, are almost completely isolated from one another and hence there is no over-all rhythmic-melodic coherence.

Looking at these matters from another point of view, it should be observed that most groupings are only partially segregated from those which precede or follow them. And when we speak about the organization of a particular group, we are referring to its dominant or manifest rhythm, but not to all the rhythmic relationships in which the group is involved. Thus, concurrent with the manifest iambic organization in Examples 3–6, there exists a *latent* trochaic organization (indicated by the inverted brackets) which plays an important role in linking the iambic groups to one another and creating an over-all melodic-rhythmic pattern. And it is in part the obliteration of this latent trochaic rhythm which makes for the nearly chaotic atomization present in Example 11.

Both the composer and the performer must therefore beware of overarticulating the lower architectonic levels at the expense of the higher ones. One should articulate the smaller units only as much as is necessary to make the musical intention clear. Added articulation, while it will change the character of the music (and this is of course important in one's interpretation), may well weaken the phrasing of larger parts without appreciably strengthening the grouping of the smaller ones.

AMPHIBRACH, ANAPEST, AND DACTYL IN DUPLE METER

Because the folk tune being used is organized into two-unit groups (trochees or iambs), it cannot give rise to three-unit rhythms (anapests, dactyls, or amphibrachs) without more substantial temporal alterations than have been employed heretofore. That is, in order for there to be three-unit groups in $\frac{2}{4}$ meter, two of the quarter-notes must be replaced by a single half-note, thus:

$$\underset{-\ \cup\ \cup}{\flat\ \flat\flat}\ ,\ \underset{\cup\ -\ \cup}{\flat\flat\ \flat}\ ,\ ,\ \text{or}\ \underset{\cup\ \cup\ -}{\flat\flat\ \flat}\ ,$$

THE INFLUENCE OF MELODY

Example 12 is an instance of amphibrach grouping. The upbeat is necessary, since without it the grouping would probably be interpreted as anapestic. With it, the grouping is amphibrach throughout, because, as has been mentioned, once a rhythm is established, it tends to perpetuate itself. However, despite the upbeat, the initial amphibrach grouping is rather unstable. For the final note of the rhythm (the D) tends, because of similarity and proximity, to group itself with the D which follows rather than with the G with which it properly belongs but from which it is separated in pitch.

EXAMPLE 12

The impression of amphibrach grouping is therefore appreciably strengthened if, as in Example 13, the afterbeat is changed from D to B. Not only is the afterbeat now closer to the accent, but the second group is more clearly segregated from the first.

Of course, the performer, interpreting this as an amphibrach rhythm, will automatically phrase in such a way that this grouping will be clear. He will, as indicated in Example 14, make minute temporal adjustments, bringing the unaccented beats closer to the accent and cutting some of the value of the afterbeat by playing it staccato. This will create both coherence within groups and separation between them. Particularly in cases such as this where the upbeat is closer

EXAMPLE 13

EXAMPLE 14

in pitch to the accent than the afterbeat is, the performer will, by slightly stressing the accent, tie the afterbeat to the accent. And finally he will probably group the accent and the beat which follows it by playing them legato.

THE INFLUENCE OF HARMONY

Example 15, an anapestic rhythm, is of particular interest because it illustrates the influence of rhythmic grouping on the melodic-harmonic organization of music. Observe, first of all, that one does not feel relaxed and easy when the tune is performed in this way. The tension present in performing Example 15

EXAMPLE 15

EXAMPLE 16

is quite apparent if we compare it with Example 16, which uses the same pitches and the same grouping but in a different order. Example 15 seems relatively strained (and of course this may be precisely what the composer desires) because it emphasizes a melodic-harmonic pattern which is at odds with the simple tonic character of the tune. That is, the rhythm emphasizes the subdominant side of G major by making the tones E, C, and A structural points in the melody. Example 16, on the other hand, seems relaxed and natural because its rhythm supports the tonic character of the tune, emphasizing the tones D, B, and G.

Notice that though the original barring of the tune has been maintained in Example 16, the change in rhythm and the resulting change in melodic emphasis have created a change in metric organization. The opening tones should now be written as upbeats to the D, as in Example 17.

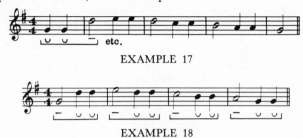

EXAMPLE 17

EXAMPLE 18

Actually the temporal-melodic arrangement given in Example 15 can be made to seem relaxed and natural harmonically simply by changing the rhythmic grouping from an anapest to a dactyl, as shown in Example 18. Now the half-notes are heard not as structural points toward which other notes move, but as appoggiaturas which themselves tend toward structural tones, and thus the fundamentally triadic character of the folk tune is maintained.

THE INFLUENCE OF STRESS

It was pointed out in chapter i that while a stress does not change the function of a beat within the pulse continuum—an unaccented beat remains unaccented even if stressed with a sforzando—stress, whether on accented or unaccented beats, generally changes the grouping of the unaccented beats. More specifically, a stress tends to indicate the beginning of a group.[2]

EXAMPLE 19

Indeed, the reader may have noticed that in performing Example 18 he stressed the half-notes. Without stresses to mark the beginning of groups, durational differences such as are present here would tend to produce end-accented rhythms (see pp. 10–11). Thus one way of indicating the desired dactylic grouping to the performer would be to mark the accented half-notes sforzando, as in Example 19.

Similarly in Example 20, which resembles Example 4, though the rhythm of

---

[2] The sign "/" will be used to indicate stress. Thus ∠ indicates a stressed accent and ◡́ indicates a stressed weak beat.

the tune would for melodic reasons normally be interpreted as iambic, the grouping can be changed from end-accented to beginning-accented if a stress is placed on the accented beats.

EXAMPLE 20

Conversely, in order to achieve the iambic grouping indicated in Example 6, the reader probably found himself stressing the weak beats which mark the beginning of each group. In fact, were the tune written with stresses, as shown in Example 21, the iambic rhythm would probably be clear without the detailed expression marks indicated in Example 6.

EXAMPLE 21

Observe that in each of these instances the reversal or inversion of the grouping gives a special flavor or character to the tune. It feels somewhat tense and constrained because without the stress the melodic-temporal organization would give rise to a different, more natural, rhythmic pattern. The stress is, so to speak, an external force imposed upon the pattern, changing its normal behavior.

THE INFLUENCE OF ORNAMENTATION

Thus far stress has been considered as a product of dynamic intensification. But there is another way in which a beat may receive stress, namely, through ornamentation. Indeed, in many cases ornamentation seems to function like stress in the articulation of rhythmic groupings.

Ornaments or embellishments act to emphasize tones in several ways. First, if an accented note is a non-chord tone, as in the case of the appoggiatura, its tendency to move to a consonance makes it feel "heavy" or stressed. This is the case with the E in Example 12 and the first C-sharp in Example 31. It is interesting to note in the latter example that the appoggiatura effect continues even where, as in measure 4, the "appoggiatura" *is* actually a chord tone. Indeed the appoggiatura pattern as a melodic-rhythmic phenomenon is so firmly established in this style that it may arise in the absence of dissonance simply because a note has been preceded by an anticipation—because it sounds like a prepared dissonance—as in Example 30*b*.

A grace note may stress a substantive note because it approaches the substantive note by a skip—landing more heavily upon it than would a conjunct grace note. This is the case in Example 22. Note that here too the embellishments, if played in strict time, tend to delay the arrival of the substantive tone, making it seem stressed when it is actually presented. It should also be observed that

EXAMPLE 22

embellishments perform a melodic function—articulating the direction of melodic expectation. Thus in Example 22 the structural gaps created by the grace notes emphasize the tendency of the melody to descend. Lastly, embellishments may serve to mark off groupings. They often have an articulatory function. This is clear in Example 22 (see also Examples 56*b*, 63, 65, 69, 98).

COMPOSITE SUBGROUPS

Examples 15–19 were designated as instances of anapestic and dacytlic rhythms. But they are so only in a qualified sense. The mind tries to group stimuli in the simplest possible way and tends whenever possible to equalize the accented and unaccented parts of a rhythm. Because of this tendency toward the equalization of elements in a group, which we shall call the Principle of Metric Equivalence, the groups in Example 15 might also be analyzed as iambs with divided upbeats— ♩ ♩ | ♩ —rather than as anapests. Similarly the groups in Example 18 might be considered trochees with divided afterbeats— ♩ ♩ ♩ — rather than as dactyls.

Thus in analyzing rhythmic organization, the most fundamental and general classification of structures would be that of end-, beginning-, and middle-accented. Changes within these types, say from iamb to anapest, are as a rule much less striking than are changes between them as long as meter is constant. However, neither changes within such classifications nor the special organization of a given grouping should be slighted. Indeed, what for the musician is most important of all is precisely the unique interrelationship of melody, temporal organization, stress, and other factors which give a particular rhythm its peculiar character and mode of progression.

How an upbeat is comprehended—whether as a single unit or as subdivided and articulated—depends upon tempo as well as upon the particular organization of the musical materials. For instance, if Example 17 is played at a rapid tempo, then the weak beats will tend to be heard as a pair of upbeats to a single downbeat—that is, the whole group will be perceived as an anapest. If, on the other hand, the tempo is very slow, the mind will tend to impose an organization upon the weak beats and establish a relationship between them, creating a trochaic subgroup which is anacrustic to the main accent, thus: 𝅘𝅥 𝅘𝅥 𝅗𝅥 .

The articulation of the grouping in such a composite upbeat can be emphasized by giving the anacrusis a distinctive melodic-temporal shape—a rhythmic organization of its own—as in Example 23a and b. Indeed, in Example 23b the anacrusis is even further subdivided.

EXAMPLE 23

These changes not only modify the character of the rhythm within the upbeat group itself but they also influence the quality of the downbeat D, which now appears more strongly emphasized than before. This occurs because the more marked the temporal differentiation is—the shorter the note values of the upbeat relative to the downbeat—the stronger the stress on the accented note. Notice also that in Example 23b the final two sixteenth-notes are both part of the upbeat group and form a sort of extra anacrusis to the D. They are, so to speak, an upbeat within an upbeat and, as we shall presently see, they serve in addition as a rhythmic pivot welding the anacrustic group to the accent.

The force of the accent can be still further intensified if the anacrusis is incomplete, as in Example 24. Since the chief accent of the anacrusis is missing, there is no stable trochaic organization as in Example 23. The group is incomplete and hence rushes toward the downbeat which serves as the goal of the upbeat group.

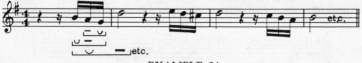

EXAMPLE 24

Through the intensification of the anacrustic function of the upbeat, the accent becomes particularly marked because durational differences are strongly emphasized by the brevity of the upbeat relative to the accent.

DACTYL, ANAPEST, AND AMPHIBRACH IN TRIPLE METER

Looking back over the changes to which an innocent tune has been subjected, the reader will observe that every type of rhythm is possible in duple meter. However, not all are achieved with equal ease. Because of the operation of the

Principle of Metric Equivalence, it was difficult to create unequivocal anapests and dactyls in duple meter. Furthermore, we noted that because a three-unit group in duple time necessarily requires durational differentiation and such differences tend to produce end-accented groups, dactylic groupings could arise only if the accented beat was strongly stressed (Example 19). To study these rhythms in what might be called their "natural habitat" as well as to explore still further the intricacies and subtleties of grouping, we turn now to a tune in triple meter.

THE INFLUENCE OF MELODY, DURATION, AND STRESS

The naturalness of a dactyl grouping in triple meter is apparent in Example 25. The beginning-accented grouping of this example is a result of several aspects of the organization: (1) The note following the accent belongs to the same harmony as the accent and tends therefore to group with it. (2) The falling inflection is

EXAMPLE 25

heard as strong-weak. (3) The basic melodic line comes on the first beat of each measure—D–B–A–B—and the weak beats are heard almost as a separate figure, a kind of "umpah," beat accompaniment. Hence the G is not heard as moving to the A, but as hanging from the B.

Another important factor in articulating the groups as dactyls is the melodic disjunction between measures 2 and 3. For though there is less pitch segregation between measures 2 and 3 than within them, this change of direction is nevertheless a point of melodic, and consequently of rhythmic, separation. That is, because the motion from measure 1 to measure 2 is descending, the turning back to

EXAMPLE 26

the A is heard as a break in the melodic continuum. Furthermore, because the motion from measure 1 to measure 2 is descending, the anacrustic function of the final eighth-notes of measure 1 is not as forceful as might otherwise be the case.

The importance of the melodic structure of the first measure becomes apparent if it is rewritten as in Example 26. Now there is a rising motion from measure 1 to 2 and the anacrustic function of the eighth-notes tends to order subsequent patterns because of the parallelism between the motion from measure 1 to 2 and from measure 2 to 3. The grouping becomes ambiguous and might be middle-accented (as in *a*), or end-accented (as in *b*), as well as beginning-accented (as in Example 25). The interpretation of the performer would here be the deciding factor.

But even without this modification, the tune can be heard as a series of anapests. If it is heard in this way, the reader will probably find himself placing some stress on the second beat of the measure and making a crescendo to the accent, since such stress will articulate the grouping and the crescendo will indicate the goal of the group. Had the composer desired this rhythm he might have written the tune with a sforzando on the first of these notes and a crescendo. Of course an anapestic grouping could be achieved in other ways as well—by assigning each group to a different instrument, by providing an accompaniment figure which had such a rhythm, by playing one group forte and another piano, and so forth.

It is again important to observe that, while such a grouping is possible, the particular character of the rhythm is a result of the fact that the anapest foot is, so to speak, imposed upon a melodic organization which is more naturally dactylic. The strain in the grouping is particularly noticeable between measures 2 and 3, which we have already discussed, and between measures 3 and 4, where the marked pitch segregation tends to make for rhythmic separation. Thus the character of the anapestic grouping can be made to seem more natural and relaxed by changing the melodic motion between measures 1 and 2, so that the following measure proceeds in a like manner, and by changing the melodic progression from measure 3 to 4 so that proximate pitch progression makes grouping more relaxed. This is done in Example 27. The anapest effect will be

EXAMPLE 27

further strengthened if the initial foot is an anapest—if two quarter-notes, G, are imagined as preceding the opening D.

Although no special articulation (sforzando, instrumental change, etc.) is now required to project the desired grouping, the performer will, as we have seen before, make the anapest clear in his performance. He will tend to place the up-beats closer to the accent than he would in articulating a dactylic grouping, thus making the separation between groups more apparent, and he will very likely make a slight crescendo on the weak beats so that their relation to the accent which follows is unmistakable.

The rhythmic groups of this tune can also be heard as amphibrachs (Example 28). In this case, however, there is a tendency to stress the second tone of the group, the accent, rather than the initial upbeat. This is done because, while the melodic-temporal proximity of the upbeat to the accent makes this part of the grouping clear, there would be a tendency, were it not for the stress, for the non-proximate afterbeats to group themselves with the next upbeat to which they are closer in pitch.

EXAMPLE 28

In other situations where the proximity of the afterbeat makes its relationship to the accent clear, but in which the function of the upbeat might be in doubt, the stress is placed on the beginning of the group. This is what takes place in the third movement of Haydn's Symphony No. 104 in D Major (Example 29). Here,

EXAMPLE 29

were it not for the sforzandos placed on the upbeats, the groupings might, in spite of the initial anacrusis, have been heard as dactyls.

Without phrase or dynamic markings no musician would play Example 25 as an amphibrach, for its melodic shape makes dactylic rhythm almost a necessity. Only if the tune is modified will its rhythms be apprehended as amphibrachs. This is done in Example 30a by making the upbeat of each group closer in time

EXAMPLE 30

to its downbeat, and this also separates the end of one group from the beginning of the next. In Example 30b amphibrach groups arise naturally because the up-beats are now closer in pitch to the downbeats which follow and because the parallelism between the first two amphibrachs is made clear. Obviously these modes of articulation could be combined, reinforcing one another.

THE CHARACTER OF PARTICULAR RHYTHMS

As one sings or plays over Examples 28, 30a, and 30b one becomes aware again of the diversity of rhythmic character and mode of progression which can arise within the same grouping and even the same basic musical structure. Example 28, for instance, tends to be thumping and somewhat ponderous, like a peasant dance, because, if the amphibrach rhythm is to predominate, the accents must be heavily stressed. Example 30*b* seems, by comparison, light and almost lilting, for the groupings are not strained and require no special stress for their articulation. On the other hand, the brevity of the anacrusis relative to the remainder of the group makes Example 30*a* seem uneven and rather coarse. The simplicity and regularity of the melodic-harmonic structure of this tune calls for an even beat, and the abbreviated anacrusis seems both contrived, overarticulating the pattern, and hurried, because it arrives too late. Also contributing to the rather blatant character of this organization is the undue emphasis which the accent receives as a result of the shortened upbeat. The passage is obvious, almost vulgar.

By way of illustrating how very different the effects arising within one type of rhythmic grouping can be, let us examine another of Haydn's themes, one from the Finale of the "Oxford" Symphony in G Major (Example 31). This example

EXAMPLE 31

is somewhat more complex than those analyzed heretofore. On the lower architectonic levels the weak beats, functioning as pivots (as both afterbeats and upbeats), so fuse the first five eighth-notes that decisive groupings cannot be made without doing violence to the pattern. This is true of the quarter-note motion (Example 32, analysis *b*) as well as of the eighth-note motion (Example 32, analysis *a*). Because these eighth-notes are apprehended as a cohesive group, the manifest rhythm is that of the whole motive and, as indicated in Example 31, the grouping of this rhythm is an amphibrach.

EXAMPLE 32

The witty and somewhat impertinent—almost brusque—character of this theme is in large part a result of the durational disproportion among the units of the main rhythmic group. The extended anacrusis leads one to expect a longer final unit. Not only is the accent too short, in relation to the upbeat group, but the weak afterbeat is even shorter. The second motive seems to begin too soon, interrupting, as it were, the natural duration of the initial motive. Thus each group embodies in itself a kind of composed accelerando, each unit of the grouping being shorter than the one which precedes it. And this quickening of the pace is carried through into the last two measures, where the amphibrach groupings come twice as fast.

If one compares the theme given in Example 31 with the tune, "Twinkle, Twinkle, Little Star," one finds that both have the same fundamental melodic motion, save in the final two measures. This is shown in Example 33, in which the folk tune is written in an amphibrach rhythm (with an anacrusis added) for the sake of comparison. The vast difference between the effects of the two tunes

EXAMPLE 33

arises from the asymmetrical proportions of the Haydn compared to the symmetrical proportions of the folk tune, as well as from the vital melodic differences, for example, the appoggiatura in measure 2 of the Haydn.

Notice that in order to make the folk tune reach a semicadence and thus conform to the motion of the Haydn theme, the final measure has been rewritten. As with the Haydn, this final measure now seems faster than the earlier ones because more takes place in the same amount of time. To put the matter somewhat differently, Haydn's tune is so composed that it avoids the lifeless regularity of motion and the letdown of expectation which occur if there is a cadence on the tonic. And had the final two measures of the Haydn been written as in Example 33*b*, this would certainly have been the case.

In addition to posing new problems, these last analyses have been introduced to emphasize two general considerations. First, the primary focus of attention should be upon the individuality of the particular rhythmic organization being analyzed. The theories and classifications presented are a means toward more sensitive musical understanding, not ends pursued for their own sakes. Thus, while differences may, as we have seen, be made more apparent by a comparison of tunes which are in some respects similar, the difference between rhythms is much more important than their similarity—the fact, for instance, that both are amphibrach rhythms. Second, the great importance of small changes in temporal relationships should make both the performer and the critic acutely conscious of the delicate decisions that must be made in the interpretation and analysis of music. Grouping, or phrasing, often is very subtle and requires sensitivity, experience, and understanding.

IAMB AND TROCHEE IN TRIPLE METER

THE INFLUENCE OF MELODY, DURATION, AND STRESS

Let us now return to our variations on the tune "Ach du lieber Augustin."

An iambic version can be created simply by making temporal differentiation such that the upbeat is clearly proximate to the accent (Example 34a). Once

EXAMPLE 34

again, however, the large skip between measures 3 and 4 makes the end-accented grouping seem rather strained. The rhythmic pattern is more relaxed if the melodic and harmonic groupings are congruent, as in Example 34b. Note, too, that the end-accented impression is improved if the tune is imagined with an upbeat G in front of the first measure.

The reader will remember that it was difficult to achieve a dactylic grouping in ¼ time because here a three-unit group requires temporal differentiation and hence tends to be end-accented. A similar situation obtains with regard to the trochee in triple meter. When a triple meter is organized into two-unit groups, there will necessarily be temporal differentiation and the resulting rhythm will tend to be end-accented, as in Example 34. However, as in the case of the dactyl in duple meter, this naturally end-accented organization can be made beginning-accented if the accented note is sufficiently stressed (Example 35).

EXAMPLE 35

INVERTED GROUPS

There is, however, another way in which a trochaic group can be found in triple meter—namely, through what we shall call "group inversion," where the accented beat is shorter than the unaccented one (Example 36). Such rhythms are sometimes referred to as "Scotch snaps."

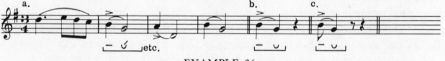

EXAMPLE 36

Here the longer weak beat acts to complete the group. And if the unaccented beat is followed by a rest, as in Example 36b and c, the temporal separation makes the groupings even more incisive. Notice that once again one tends to place added stress upon the beginning of the group, the accent, in order to make the rhythm as clear as possible. And as the accent becomes shorter in relation to the underlying pulse, segregation of groups becomes more marked and the stress placed upon the accent heavier.

The weak beat of an inverted trochee, unlike that of a normal trochee, does not tend to become a pivot, functioning first as the afterbeat of a trochee and then as the upbeat of an iamb or an amphibrach. This is partly because of its relative proximity to the preceding accent (and its concomitant separation from the following beat) and partly because it is both stabilized and emphasized by its relative length. Furthermore, owing to this emphasis as well as to the fact that it is not part of a cadential progression, the weak beat, though it ends the group, does not feel like a feminine ending. Inverted trochees are thus peculiarly cohesive and, as a result, it is the total group rather than any one of its components which acts as the unit of motion. This becomes very clear if we compare the opening of the third movement of Beethoven's Piano Concerto in B-flat with its inverted trochees (Example 37a) to a variant in which the weak beat is shorter than the accent (Example 37b). In the former the groups are clearly defined and precisely articulated, while in the latter the groups are blurred, flowing into one another.

EXAMPLE 37

Related to the inverted trochee is the "closed" trochee in which the accented part of the group, though equal in duration to the weak part, is made up of several short notes— ♩♩♩ Because it is composed of short notes moving to the weak beat, the accent is made proximate to and emphasizes the weak beat. And the closed group, rather than any part of it, constitutes the unit of motion. Thus while the trochaic grouping is very clear in the fragment from the "Laudamus Te" of Bach's Mass in B Minor (Example 37c), it is less clear in the variants (d and e) in which the weak beats have an "on-going" motion—a tendency to become anacruses. This tendency would have been considerably strengthened had the sense of harmonic change, which segregates the groups, been less marked. Such patterns are particularly common in Baroque music, where, apparently because of their precision, they are used frequently, both written out and in the form of ornaments such as the *Schleifer* and the mordent.

The inverted temporal relationships present in Example 36 might be still further varied by placing a stress followed by a crescendo on the unaccented notes, thus creating an inverted iamb (Example 38). As before (see Example 26), the melodic line of the first measure has been varied to emphasize the end-accented grouping. However, because the rather gauche, lopsided humor of the unstable iamb was what was desired, the final measures have not been modified (as they were in Example 34*b*) to make them more naturally iambic.

EXAMPLE 38

EXAMPLE 39

It is more difficult to invert a dactyl, a three-unit group, in duple meter because the desire for metric equivalence tends to make the beat which is divided (and one of them must necessarily be so) seem like a subgroup of a larger two-unit rhythm. That is, the whole group will appear to be a trochee with a divided first unit rather than a genuine three-unit dactyl (Example 39*a*).

Only by forcing the mind to perceive the group as a three-unit one will we find an unequivocal inverted dactyl arising in duple meter. As shown in Example 39*b*, this can be accomplished through syncopation. However, even with this temporal organization a dactylic rhythm will arise only if the first note of the group receives the stress necessary to tie the following beats to it. For if the initial beat is not thus stressed, the final note of the measure tends to split off and become grouped with the following accent, forming a partially inverted amphibrach (Example 39*c*).

The dactylic feeling of Example 39*a* can be intensified by subdividing the first two beats of the group, making them into more clearly separate entities (Example 40*a*). But even here it is possible to perceive the rhythm as trochaic. However, if the tune is written in triple meter (Example 40*b*), then the inverted dactyl is more patent.

Example 39c was said to be "partially inverted" because only the second and third units of the group are in reverse order—short-long. In a fully inverted amphibrach the upbeat would be longer than the downbeat and the downbeat shorter than the afterbeat (Example 40c).

A properly devised syncopation will also give rise to an inverted anapest (Example 41a). However, in order for this variant to be perceived as an anapest, the

EXAMPLE 40

EXAMPLE 41

beat must be felt in twos and the tempo must be rather fast. Otherwise, because of the desire to make the organization as simple as possible, a subgroup will arise within the anacrusis, making the over-all rhythm seem to be iambic with a divided upbeat rather than really anapestic (Example 41b).

These considerations would seem to indicate that, for purposes of analysis, two different aspects of syncopation should be distinguished. On the one hand, in syncopations of well-articulated rhythmic-melodic patterns occurring between voices, the relationships and problems involved are primarily metric. On the other hand, in periodic syncopations within a single voice, such as we have been discussing, the relationships and problems involved are primarily rhythmic. Of course, some continuous syncopations, such as those in which suppressed accents produce extended anacruses, are also aspects of rhythm. Needless to say, the interpretation of a syncopation—whether as rhythmic, metric, or a combination of both—has an important effect upon performance, since it will modify the placement of beats, the amount and placement of stress, the phrasing, and so forth. (The problem of syncopation is discussed more fully in chapter iv.)

RHYTHMIC AMBIGUITY

In the examples thus far presented the rhythmic organization, however complex, was clear and incisive. But this is not invariably the case. Often the rhythm is ambiguous and it is difficult to decide which grouping is the dominant or manifest one. For instance, in Example 42, a tune similar in many ways to

"Ach du lieber Augustin," the melodic uniformity of the second and third measures makes it possible to interpret the groups as amphibrachs, dactyls, or perhaps even anapests. Thus if the rhythm is *thought* of as being dactylic, the performer will unconsciously play the tune in such a way as to make this interpretation clear, articulating the groups by means of stress, temporal displacement, dynamics, and the like. But if the rhythm is *thought* of as being amphibrach, performance will make this grouping the manifest one.

EXAMPLE 42

The equivocal grouping on the primary level is partly a result of the character of the melodic line. Specifically, the focal tone of the third measure might be G, with the first A an appoggiatura and the second A a passing-note to be B. In this case the rhythm would probably be amphibrach, as indicated in analysis *a*. Or the focal tone might be the A, the harmony on the dominant, the G a changing-note. The rhythm would then be dactylic, as in analysis *b*. An anapestic grouping is unlikely because the second B in measure 2 is heard as an afterbeat of the first B and does not easily form the beginning of a new group. Only by replacing this B with a C (as in the second phrase, measure 6) might the rhythm become anapestic. Notice, however, that this change also strengthens the dactyl impression because measure 6, like measure 7, now has a more definitive shape. Of course these ambiguities could be resolved by a decisive harmonization.

The ambiguity of the second measure of the tune is, at least from a negative point of view, also the result of the indefinite rhythmic organization of the first measure, whose second half becomes anacrustic in the middle of a beat. That is, were the grouping of the first measure decisive, it would influence that of the following measures, because, as we have noted, once a grouping is established it tends to be continued. Indeed, the influence of prior organization is particularly strong in this case precisely because of the ambiguity of the second and third measures. For instance, the presence of the upbeat, G, to measure 5 makes the second phrase seem much more end- or middle-accented than the first phrase.

Thus if the first measure is organized so that only the final beat becomes an anacrusis, then the rhythm will be amphibrach (Example 43*a*). Notice that the amphibrach impression is considerably strengthened when an upbeat (G or D) is imagined before the first measure, thus making the initial group a complete amphibrach. Or if the sense of upbeat is eliminated and if there is separation in pitch between the first two measures, isolating the groups, then the rhythm of the second measure will appear to be dactylic (Example 43*b*). Finally, if the first measure is written so that the last two quarter-notes form an anacrusis to measure 2, then the following measures tend to be heard as anapests (Example 43*c*).

EXAMPLE 43

Observe that were the same changes made in the first measure of "Ach du lieber Augustin," their influence upon the organization of the succeeding measures would be noticeably smaller. Because the rhythmic-melodic shapes of "Ach du lieber Augustin" are more decisively and patently structured, they are less readily influenced by prior rhythmic groupings than the tune in Example 42, which, at least on the lowest architectonic level, is without a very strong rhythmic personality or profile.

The words "well-structured and decisive" or "weak and ambiguous" should not be understood to imply any valuations. Ambiguous rhythms have their own character and function and play just as important a role in shaping musical experience as do unambiguous incisive rhythmic shapes. The smoothly lyrical line of the tune in Example 42 is a result of the fact that the rhythmic groups flow into one another. So is the correlative feeling that each phrase of the tune constitutes a single, unbroken musical pattern. Conversely, the heavily marked, dance-like thumping of "Ach du lieber Augustin" results partly from the sharp separation of the groups from one another. The tune seems for this reason to be a compound of almost independent motives.

EXAMPLE 44

Furthermore, these differences are not confined to the initial phrases of each tune. They become even more emphatic as the tunes progress. Thus in the second part of "Ach du lieber" the separateness of quasi-independent motives becomes the basis for musical progression (Example 44), while in the second part of the other tune the ambiguous overlapping of groups is, as we shall see, the principle of construction.

Now the reader may ask: if I have a choice—if I can interpret the rhythm of a tune as an anapest, an amphibrach, or a dactyl—how do I decide which way it *should* be performed? What is the correct way? In the light of what has just been said, the answer in this case would seem to be that the passage should not be decisively "interpreted" as any particular grouping. However, though the articulation of the rhythm should not be made as patent and forceful as that of "Ach du lieber Augustin," groupings are nonetheless possible and necessary because, were the phrase performed with exaggerated uniformity, the effect of the sequence in the second part of the tune, whose *raison d'être* is uniformity, would unquestionably be weakened.

The amphibrach grouping, given in Example 42 (analysis *a*) is possible because the repeated B creates a desire for motion and change and the performer, knowing that such a change is about to take place, will group the final beat of measure 2 with the following tones—that is, he will make the B an anacrusis. Once this grouping is established, it tends to be continued and consequently determines the grouping of the following measure. The discontinuity and disturbance which would be created by a change of rhythm is out of keeping with the prevailing regularity and simplicity of this melody.

A dactylic grouping is also possible. Such a grouping would of course alter the character of the tune, making the accent somewhat more strongly stressed. But this is not necessarily bad. The choice of interpretation is up to the performer. There is no right or wrong here—just differences. However, although more than one conception of a musical phrase or passage may be correct, some are clearly wrong. For instance, an anapestic grouping of this tune would definitely be in poor taste, since it would require a noticeable stress upon the weak second beat and a crescendo to the following accent. Such an alteration would conflict with the childlike directness of the melody.

While articulation of grouping is desirable in the first two phrases of this tune, decisive articulation is out of place in the middle part (Example 45*a*). Any at-

EXAMPLE 45

tempt to divide the passage into separate rhythmic groups does violence to musical sense. Thus a clear amphibrach disturbs the continuity of the phrase (Example 45*b*); so does an unambiguous anapest (Example 45*c*); while a marked dactyl obviously distorts the general anacrustic motion of the sequence (Example 45*d*). The phrase is uniform, running without break from beginning to end. This passage is an example of a well-structured metric organization which lacks a definable rhythm.

From a theoretical point of view, what happens is that the second and perhaps the third beat of each measure act as pivots, functioning both as the end of an amphibrach and the beginning of an anapest (Example 45*a*). The successive groups are thus linked together in a smooth, unbroken series whose articulation takes place only when the goal of the series—the D—is reached. Though frequently used in this way to create ambiguity by fusing successive groups, rhythmic pivots have, as we shall see, another no less important function in the structuring of higher architectonic levels.

We have been treating this tune as an instrumental melody instead of a song. Obviously when it is sung to a text, as it is in the first act of *Hänsel und Gretel*, articulation is almost inevitable, particularly since each note is set to a separate syllable. In fact, in order to strengthen the articulation in the second half of the tune, Humperdinck feels it is necessary to place grace notes on the accented beats.

THE INFLUENCE OF RHYTHM ON MELODIC MOTION

Throughout this chapter the influence of melodic organization upon rhythmic grouping has been emphasized. For this reason it seems important to note that the converse of this is also true; rhythmic grouping may play a significant role in shaping melodic experience. Indeed, one of the values of rhythmic analysis lies in the fact that it can increase our understanding of melody. However, since this problem is peripheral to the central purpose of this book, the point will be illustrated only briefly. Example 46 presents the opening measures of Chopin's Preludes Op. 24 No. 1 and No. 4. In many ways the two are quite

EXAMPLE 46

similar. Both begin on the fifth degree of the scale. Both contain marked temporal differentiation. In both, the short, final note of the measure is a non-chord tone, a kind of changing-note. But in rhythm these two melodies are very different.

In spite of marked temporal differentiation and proximity of pitch, the melody of the first Prelude does not have an end-accented rhythm. The rest at the beginning of each measure separates the groups from one another, creating a trochaic grouping within each measure. And one of the things which give this Prelude its agitated, unstable character is precisely that a temporal organization which is naturally end-accented has been forced to become beginning-accented.

Because the pattern is trochaic, we are made to hear the G moving to the A, rather than the other way around. That is, we hear the melodic-rhythmic group move upward. It points in a definite direction; and when the melody does move, it fulfils our expectations. It rises.

In the fourth Prelude, on the other hand, the accent is stated in the melody and consequently the group is able to follow its natural course—to become end-accented. This iambic group, moving across the bar line from C to B rather than the reverse, begins a descending motion which we expect to be continued. And after some delay it is. The iambic grouping in this Prelude is, of course, supported by the initial anacrusis, just as the trochaic grouping of the first Prelude is supported by the lack of one.

There are of course other factors involved in shaping our expectations about melodic motion. For instance, the skip at the beginning of the fourth Prelude leads us to expect a descending line which will fill in this structural gap. And the difference in mode makes it unlikely that Prelude No. 4 will ascend, will overcome the downward tendency of the semitone. Conversely, once the motion to the sixth step of the scale has been achieved in major—as it is in Prelude No. 1— it is likely that it will move on up. But the presence of these other factors does not detract from the importance of rhythm in shaping subsequent melodic motion.

Finally, in both Preludes the latent as well as the manifest rhythms have melodic and rhythmic consequences later on. In Prelude No. 1 the latent end-accented temporal organization breaks through and becomes the manifest organization as the piece rises to its climax (measures 17–20). In Prelude No. 4 the legato melody and accompaniment, together with the temporal proximity within measures, create a rather marked latent trochaic grouping implying the possibility of upward melodic movement. The implications of the latent grouping are in fact realized progressively: first, in measure 9, then in measure 12, and at the climax of the Prelude (measures 16–18).

RECAPITULATION AND ILLUSTRATION

Perhaps the best way to summarize the materials presented in this chapter is to examine particular examples from the literature of music which clearly illustrate the various rhythmic structures discussed. The examples will be presented according to groupings, and within each grouping the simplest, most obvious illustrations will appear first. The discussion will be confined to essentials. Where only the melody is given, the reader should consult the original score to discover the ways in which the particular grouping is supported by such factors as harmony, texture, orchestration, and so forth. Often other instances of the rhythmic pattern being discussed are cited. The reader is urged to study and analyze these.

TROCHEE IN DUPLE METER

The theme of the fourth movement of Haydn's String Quartet Op. 33 No. 3 is trochaic on both the first and second levels (Example 47*a*). It does not seem necessary to analyze the subprimary level (i), because this motion is absorbed into the general trochaic motion of the other levels. The accompaniment, which comes on the beat, provides a slight stress that helps to enforce the trochaic organization of the second level as well as the iambic grouping of the third level. The theme, which might otherwise have been too static, is given a slight tension by the instability of the six-four harmony. And it is worth observing that when the tune comes back (measure 72) after a "Grand Pause," the tonic chord is in root position.

EXAMPLE 47

This theme furnishes an interesting instance of the importance of seemingly insignificant details. The sixteenth-notes do not change the rhythm of the primary level; nor do they alter the essential melodic motion. That is, the eighth-notes G and E could have continued throughout the theme without changing its basic structure. What then is the function of the sixteenth-note figures? One is tempted to answer that they create variety. But such an answer is only a plausible platitude. There are countless ways of achieving variety. What is crucial is the way in which the particular form of variety shapes musical experience. In this case the particular way in which the figure is elaborated at the beginning of measure 2 and in the following measures determines the grouping on the second and third rhythmic levels. For instance, had the theme been written as in Example 47*b*, the second level would have consisted of two iambs and an amphibrach; and the third level would probably have been anapestic.

The theme of Beethoven's Bagatelle Op. 119 No. 10 (Example 48) illustrates the important role which harmony often plays in the articulation of rhythm. Without the dissonances in measures 1, 3, 4, 5, 7, and 8 which make us perceive the accent as resolving to the weak beat, this theme might have been perceived as end-accented—or at least as ambiguous.

EXAMPLE 48

The sixth variation of Brahms's *Variations on a Theme by Haydn*, Op. 56a (Example 49), demonstrates the importance of stress in the articulation of beginning-accented groupings. For without the stresses, whether "composed" as in the first measure or indicated by the mark ">" in the following measures, a temporal organization such as this would tend to be heard and performed as end-accented (iambic). The trochaic organization is supported and assured by Brahms's orchestration.

EXAMPLE 49

In the trochaic groupings discussed thus far, the temporal organization has been such that, were it not for harmonic progression, orchestration, or stress, the weak beat of the group might easily have become an anacrusis to the next accent. Such groups are "open" in the sense that they have an "on-going" quality enabling them to link easily with subsequent rhythms. However, where the accented part of the trochee is divided so that it is faster than, and moves to, the weak part of the group, the trochee is stable and "closed"; the weak part of the group does not tend to become an upbeat (see pp. 30–31).

The opening measures of the third movement of Handel's Concerto Grosso No. 8 in C Minor (Example 50a) is a clear example of such a closed trochee. This is so for both the subprimary and the primary levels, since the accented beat on the primary level is faster than the weak beat. As with most echo effects the second level too is trochaic.

Although in the closed trochee the accent and the weak beat are equal in duration, the effect of the group is similar to that of the inverted trochee and should perhaps be classed with it. Example 50*b*, from the third movement of Haydn's String Quartet Op. 54 No. 3, is an illustration of an inverted trochee on the subprimary level.

EXAMPLE 50

For further study: Beethoven, Piano Trio Op. 1 No. 3, iv, 9–20; Serenade Op. 25, vi, 23–30; Brahms, Rhapsody Op. 119 No. 4, 1–4; *Variations on a Theme by Handel*, i, 1–4; Chopin, Etude Op. 25 No. 5, 1–4; Nocturne Op. 37 No. 1, 41–44; Polonaise Op. 71 No. 1, 38–47; Handel, Concerto Grosso No. 5 in D Major, v, 1–4; Haydn, Symphony No. 94 in G Major, ii, 1–16; Mozart, Clarinet Quintet (K. 541), iv, 1–8; String Quartet in D Minor (K. 421), iii, 40–47; Schubert, *Moments Musicaux* Op. 94, v, 1–8; String Quartet Op. 29, ii, 1–8; Schumann, *Carnaval*, "Valse Allemande," 1–8.[3]

TROCHEE IN TRIPLE METER

As we have seen, durational differences necessarily occur when a two-unit group, such as a trochee, arises in triple meter. The two basic patterns possible are ♩ ♪ and ♪ ♩. Of the two the second, the inverted trochee, is by far the more stable, for the weak beat, which is long and consequently felt to be somewhat stressed, does not tend to become an anacrusis to the following accent.

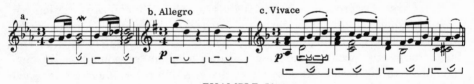

EXAMPLE 51

Example 51*a*, from the Sarabande of Bach's French Suite No. 4, is a typical instance of this pattern as it occurs in Baroque music. A somewhat different exemplification of the inverted trochee can be found in the first measures of the

---

[3] The following scheme will be used in referring to parts of musical works: The title of the work, together with whatever other identification (such as number, opus number, key, etc.) seems necessary, will be given first. Parts of works such as movements, variations, or separate pieces included within one title will be designated by small roman numerals: i, ii, etc. Measure numbers will be given in arabic numerals: 1–8.

Minuet of Mozart's String Quartet in G Major (K. 387). Even though a rest follows the second beat in this case (Example 51*b*), the group is inverted, because the weak second beat is, so to speak, maintained in the mind of the listener. However, since its literal duration is normal, it does not tend to receive the slight stress which is generally felt to accompany the weak unit of the inverted trochee.

Since the inverted (short-long) effect of this kind of pattern is emphasized when the accent is divided (Example 51*a*), this procedure is, as one would expect, quite common. What is less common is the division of the second part of the inverted trochee into smaller note values. But this is precisely what occurs in the second movement of Brahms's Sonata in A Major for Violin and Piano (Example 51*c*). Though the actualization of the third beat of the measure would seem necessarily to produce a dactyl, ♩ ♪♪♪♪ , rather than an inverted trochee, ♩ ♪♪♪♪ , this is not the case. For the final weak beats are so strongly unified that they are perceived as constituting a single unit. That Brahms thinks of the group in this way is shown by the rhythm of the accompaniment. It is interesting to note that this inverted, somewhat forced grouping is allowed to assume a more natural pattern when a second melody is presented at measure 31.

The long-short, ♩ ♩ , trochee is much less stable, for the short weak beat has a strong tendency to become an anacrusis to the following accent. This tendency can be counteracted in two ways: (1) by placing stress upon the accent, as in Beethoven's *Overture to Egmont* (Allegro, measures 229–35; Example 52*a*) and (2) by explicitly connecting the accent to the weak beat with a series of shorter notes as in Example 52*b* from the second movement of Mozart's Horn Quintet (K. 407), measures 12–14. The first of these patterns is much less stable than the second. Indeed the strong tendency for the weak beat to become an anacrusis is realized at the end of the passage. Whether Example 52*b* should be analyzed as having a subgroup as noted in the first measure is open to question. On the whole, the simpler analysis as a single trochee seems preferable.

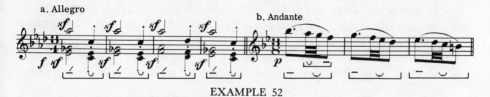

EXAMPLE 52

Just as the weak part of an inverted trochee was subdivided in Example 51*c*, so the long, accented part of a trochee is divided in the first two measures of the presto movement of Schubert's *Wanderer-Fantasie* (Example 53*a*). Because the first two beats of these measures form a single pattern and because the third and fourth measures are clearly trochaic, indicating the grouping intended by the composer, these measures have been analyzed as trochees rather than as dactyls, which they might otherwise have been thought to be. That this is the proper analysis is also shown by the stress which is placed on the first eighth-note and by the phrasing. The second pattern— ♩. ♪♩ —is perhaps the most common way of achieving a trochaic organization in triple meter. Observe, incidentally, that it is essentially the same as that of Example 52*b*.

The reader should also study measures 162–63 and 168–80 in the Scherzo of Beethoven's "Archduke" Trio, where the trochaic grouping of the same temporal organization, ♩♩♩♩ ♩, is enforced and emphasized both by the use of ornamentation and by a clearly trochaic accompaniment figure.

Example 53*b*, the opening measures of the fifth Prelude from Bach's *Twelve Little Preludes*, is interesting for several reasons. First, it emphasizes the importance

EXAMPLE 53

of metric organization in rhythmic structure. Without the time signature, $\frac{3}{4}$, the grouping might have been interpreted as being $2 \times \frac{3}{8}$, instead of $3 \times \frac{2}{8}$. The former grouping, involving exact repetition, would in a sense be simpler. But, in view of the time signature, it would be wrong. Second, it might seem, since all the notes are equal and all are part of the tonic triad, that the organization is ambiguous and should be thought of as being so. However, the simplicity of the materials both within and between measures makes such an interpretation inappropriate. The effect must be clear and direct. The most straightforward mode of organization—and this is what seems called for—as shown in the analysis, is that of a trochee with a divided accent. Furthermore, the accompaniment, emphasizing the first beat of each measure, seems to indicate that Bach intends the groups to be beginning-accented.

The third of Bach's *Six Little Preludes* (Example 54) also employs a pattern composed of six equal notes. But in this case the simple triadic organization

EXAMPLE 54

comes at the end, and hence it is the weak part of the trochee which is divided. Both the accompaniment (measures 9–11) and later melodic patterns make it clear that the basic grouping is trochaic.

For further study: Bach, English Suite No. 4, Sarabande; Sonata in C Minor for Unaccompanied Cello, Sarabande; Beethoven, Symphony No. 7, iii, 14–16 and 30–59; Chopin, Mazurka Op. 41 No. 3, 1–4; Waltz Op. 64 No. 1, 70–74; Handel, Concerto Grosso No. 2, iii, 1–6; Haydn, String Quartet Op. 55 No. 3, 1–4; Mozart, Divertimento in D Major (K. 205), ii (trio), 1–6; String Quartet in D Major (K. 575), iii, 34–37; Schumann, *Symphonic Etudes*, v, 1–4.

DACTYL IN TRIPLE METER

Although triple meter easily gives rise to the dactyl, unless melodic and temporal organization, and orchestration and stress are carefully handled, the grouping tends to be unstable—that is, the final beat tends to split away from the first beats and become an anacrusis to the following accent. For instance, the opening measures of Purcell's "Golden Sonata" for Violin and Clavier (Example 55) are unmistakable dactyls. But, for melodic and harmonic reasons and perhaps because of a fundamental tendency toward end-accentuation, the final beat of the third measure becomes an upbeat.

EXAMPLE 55

A patent and stable dactyl organization can be assured in a number of different ways. One of the most common is to subdivide either the first or the second elements of the group: ♫♩ ♩ or ♩ ♫♩. As is the case with the closed trochee, the motion thus created on the subprimary level tends to tie the group together. The "Davidsbündler" March (Example 56a) from Schumann's *Carnaval*, and the opening measures of Chopin's Mazurka Op. 56 No. 1 (Example 56b) are illustrations of this type of organization. Observe that in both

EXAMPLE 56

cases the beginning-accented organization is supported and enforced by stress or by ornamentation. In the Schumann example the sforzandi make this obvious. In the Chopin example stress is a result both of the richer sonority on the first beat of the measure and the ornamentation: the broken diad and the mordent emphasize this beat. This again supports the hypothesis that there is a close relationship between ornamentation and rhythmic organization and, more specifically, seems to indicate that in some cases stress and ornamentation perform similar functions.

A beginning-accented group can also be assured by special articulation such as one finds in the "Alla danza tedesca" (Example 57) of Beethoven's String Quartet, Op. 130. Were it not for the emphasis placed upon the second beat of the measure by the crescendo and the sixteenth-note rest at the end of the measure, there would be an almost unavoidable tendency to hear the final beat of the measure as an anacrusis. This is particularly clear in the first measure, where the motion downward through the triad makes the G a goal of motion. Note that the crescendo in the first measure by emphasizing the second beat corresponds, so to speak, to the subdivision of the beat in Example 56a and that the temporal organization of the third measure is like that of Example 56b. The character of the tune is a product of this negation of the tendency toward end-accentuation.

EXAMPLE 57

Harmony and meter can also help to enforce the impression of dactylic grouping. In Schumann's *Symphonic Etudes*, No. 9 (Example 58a), the melodic motion of the lower voices and the dominant-tonic progression in the second measure help to create clear dactyls. However, the dominant harmony at the end of the third measure makes the final beat into a rhythmic pivot (see pp. 62 ff.), an upbeat as well as an afterbeat, linking the last two measures. In "Des Abends" (Example 58b) from Schumann's *Fantasiestücke* a hemiole rhythm—2 × $\frac{3}{16}$ against 3 × $\frac{2}{16}$ —prevents the groups from becoming end-accented by placing a metric stress

EXAMPLE 58

on the point of metric coincidence—at the beginning of each group. This effect is supported by the accompaniment figure, which is a closed trochee.

Orchestration, too, can be used to prevent the final beat of a dactyl from becoming an anacrusis. For instance, the third beat, F-sharp, of the first measure of the Scherzo of Beethoven's Symphony No. 2 (Example 59a) might have been thought of as an upbeat to the following measure (Example 59b) were it not for the fact that Beethoven separates it in both range and tone color from the following accent. Observe, by the way, that Beethoven uses dynamic change to create a trochaic organization on the second level.

EXAMPLE 59

For further study: Bach, Sonata No. 6 for Violin and Clavier, iii (Allegro), 1–2 and 14–17; *Well-tempered Clavier*, Vol. I, Prelude xx, 1–4; Beethoven, String Quartet Op. 95, iii, 1–4 and 9–12; Brahms, Symphony No. 2, iii, 1–4, 106–20, and 126–55; Chopin, Mazurka Op. 50 No. 3, 45–52; Waltz Op. 18, 5–12; Handel, Concerto Grosso No. 6, v, 1–2 and 5–6; Mozart, Symphony No. 39 (K. 543), iii, 9–12; Schubert, Impromptu Op. 142 No. 4, 1–16.

DACTYL IN DUPLE METER

Dactylic grouping is not common in duple meter because, as we have seen, if the grouping is to arise, one beat of the meter must be divided: (a) ♩ ♫, (b) ♫ ♩, or (c) ♪♩ ♪. Because of the Principle of Metric Equivalence (see pp. 22–23), patterns *a* and *b* tend to be perceived as trochees with a divided weak beat, ♩ ♫, or a divided accent, ♫ ♩ .

Of the three patterns, *a* is the least easily perceived as dactylic. Because the pattern is open and "on-going," either one or both of the eighth-notes tend to become upbeats, forming groupings such as ♩ ♫ | ♩ or ♩ ♫ | ♩ ♪ . But even when the pattern remains within the measure, it is generally perceived as trochaic rather than dactylic. The long initial note, acting as a standard of measurement, tends to make the final beat seem divided. Only where the last note of the group has some independence, forming part of a new harmony or resolving an appoggiatura, will any sense of dactylic organization occur. But even in such cases the question is in doubt. Thus measures 11 and 12 of the second movement of Brahms's Violin Concero (Example 60*a*) might, as indicated in the analyses, be interpreted as either dactylic or trochaic. Tempo is clearly an important factor; the more rapid the speed of the divided beat, the greater the tendency to apprehend it as a unitary subgroup.

EXAMPLE 60

Although the tempo of the final movement of Haydn's "London" Symphony in D Major (Example 60*b*) is quite fast, its melodic-rhythmic pattern seems more dactylic. In the first place, pattern *b*, which it employs, establishes the smaller note-value—the quarter-note in this case—as the initial standard of measurement. And, second, the skip from the second quarter-note emphasizes that tone and gives it some independence. But even in this case the groups can also be analyzed as trochees with a divided accent. It should be noted that the most characteristic feature of both patterns (*a* and *b*)—the fact that they are beginning-accented—is not affected by the analysis chosen.

Only when the secondary accent is suppressed, as in pattern *c*, will an unequivocal dactyl be found in duple meter. And even then the melodic, harmonic, and orchestral organization must be such that the pattern does not become end- or middle-accented: ♩♩ ♩ │♩♩ ♩ or ♩♩ ♩ │♩♩ . For instance, in the first movement of Franck's Piano Quintet in F Minor the figure ♩ ♩ ♩ or ♫ ♩ ♩ becomes the basis of two different groupings. When it is introduced at measure 50 (Example 61*a*), the final beat of the measure moves across the bar line, forming an amphibrach. At measure 74 (Example 61*b*) this grouping becomes the basis for a rather long passage which continues to measure 90. At this point essentially the same figure gives rise to a clearly dactylic rhythm (Example 61*c*).

The reasons for the difference between the last two of these groupings are partly melodic and partly harmonic. Melodically the final beat of the measure in Example 61*b* is closer to the following accent than to the half-note which precedes it. Consequently, it tends to group with the accent. Moreover, the half-note in Example 61*b* is a note of harmonic resolution—a tone to which the preceding tones have moved. As a result it is perceived as the goal and end of a rhythm. In Example 61*c*, however, the half-note is a dissonance and the final note of the measure is its resolution. Therefore this final note is heard as the goal which

EXAMPLE 61

completes the group. Though theoretically possible, the pattern never gives rise to an end-accented grouping in this piece (for an instance of a similar temporal organization which gives rise to an end-accented grouping, see Example 70*b*, p. 52).

Example 62, from the first movement of Schumann's String Quartet Op. 41 No. 1, presents no analytical problems. It is included to illustrate the fact that a trochaic grouping can extend over several measures.

EXAMPLE 62

For further study: Bach, Suite No. 3 for Orchestra, iv, 13–16; Beethoven, *Leonore Overture No. 3* ,13 ff., 70–71, and 316 ff.; String Quartet Op. 18 No. 4, i, 5–7; Franck, Symphony in D Minor, i, 129–32 (ambiguous?); Mozart, Serenade in D Major (K. 239), i, 6–9 and 51–54; Schubert, *Wanderer-Fantasie*, Allegro, 112–19.

NORMAL IAMBS IN DUPLE AND TRIPLE METER

On lower architectonic levels the normal iamb (short-long) is a very common grouping in both duple and triple meter. When clear temporal differentiation is present, there is generally no problem of recognition and analysis. Since such rhythms do not require discussion, we will cite only a few typical instances from the literature:

Bach, Brandenburg Concerto No. 3, i:

Bach, French Suite No. 2, Gigue:

Bartók, Sonata for Two Pianos and Percussion i, 332 ff.:

Beethoven, Symphony No. 5, i:

Brahms, Symphony No. 4, i:

Chopin, Nocturne, Op. 15 No. 3, 7 ff.:

Debussy, *Nocturnes for Orchestra*, "Fêtes," 124 ff.:

Fauré, Piano Quartet Op. 15, i:

Handel, Concerto Grosso No. 4, iii:

Mozart, String Quartet in G Major (K. 387), iii:

Schumann, *Symphonic Etudes*, No. 10:

Where the temporal or melodic organization does not create a clearly iambic grouping, phrasing, instrumentation, stress, and ornamentation are often used to articulate groupings. For instance, the third measure of Example 63 (Haydn, Piano Sonata No. 37 in D Major, i), coming as it does after two measures which are clearly trochaic, would hardly be thought of as iambic were it not for the phrasing (see also Example 81, p. 65).

Similarly, in Example 64 (Beethoven, Symphony No. 5, iv, 22–25) a clear end-

Allegro con brio

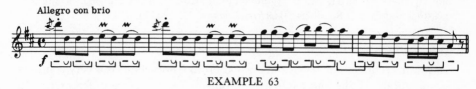

EXAMPLE 63

accented rhythm is created by the phrasing, stress, and orchestration which mark the beginning of the upbeat groups.

EXAMPLE 64

Example 65, from the fourth movement of Mozart's *Eine kleine Nachtmusik*, illustrates the important role which ornaments can play in articulating rhythm. The repeated notes in measures 33 and 34 would create trochaic groups, as they do in measure 32, except for the turn (acting almost like a sforzando) and the phrasing which force the weak beat to move toward and group with the accent that follows.

EXAMPLE 65

For further study: Beethoven, String Quartet Op. 18 No. 3, ii, 32–34; Symphony No. 9, i, 92–101; Brahms, Symphony No. 1, iv, 95–96; Chopin, Polonaise Op. 71 No. 1, 4–5; Haydn, Piano Sonata No. 33 in C Major, i, 20–40; String Quartet Op. 71 No. 1, iv, 120–25; Mozart, Symphony in B-flat Major (K. 319), iv, 114–30.

INVERTED IAMBS

The inverted iamb is not uncommon in music literature. This rhythm is, for instance, the one used in the opening melody of the third movement of Berlioz' *Symphonie fantastique* (Example 66a). It is also the rhythm of the theme of the Chaconne of Bach's Partita in D Minor for Unaccompanied Violin (Example 66b). It should be noted that the inverted iamb always requires an anacrusis

EXAMPLE 66

longer than the following accent—and the length of the accent includes any rests which may follow it. Patterns such as ♩ | ♩ ♩ | ♩ or ♩ | ♪♩ ♩ | ♪ are not really inverted iambs. In other words, to be inverted an iamb must show a disproportion between upbeat and accent, so that the accent seems to be cut short.

A distinction must be made between an inverted iamb, which in its classic form is a long, undivided upbeat moving to a shorter accent, and an extended anacrusis. In the latter, the relationship between the note-values of the upbeat and those of the accent is normal; that is, shorter notes precede longer ones. Example 67*a*, from Chopin's Nocturne Op. 48 No. 1 (measure 41), is an extended, simple anacrusis. It is like an inverted iamb in that the anacrusis, taken as a whole, is longer than the accent to which it moves.

EXAMPLE 67

Example 67*b*, from the first movement (measures 59–60) of Mozart's Serenade for Winds (K. 361), is also an extended anacrusis. But it is complex. That is, the anacrusis is made up of rhythmic groupings on several different levels. The difference between the rhythmic structures of these two examples is the result of temporal and melodic differences. Because all the elements of the Chopin anacrusis are essentially alike, groupings exist only on the lowest level. One cannot, for instance, say that the first triplet group is an upbeat to the second and third groups. Furthermore, since the passage is a "unison," neither texture nor harmony serves to create groupings above the subprimary level.

The Mozart example is quite different. It illustrates both harmonic and melodic differentiation. As a result the first three eighth-notes of the upbeat group are perceived as an anacrusis to the last four notes of the group. The anacrustic character of these last four notes is intensified both by the rhythm of the accompaniment and by the fact that the first and third notes of the group are appoggiaturas. Finally, the importance of the stress should be noted. Without the forte-piano, the pattern might have given rise to the rhythm

♩♩♩♩ ♩♩♩♩ , which would have been dull and banal. Of course, the stress does not carry the burden of articulation alone. It is supported by a change in instrumentation as well as by the phrasing.

For further study: Beethoven, String Quartet Op. 18 No. 4, ii, 20–28, 64–65, and 129–30; Symphony No. 1, ii, 49–51; Brahms, String Quintet Op. 88, ii, 26–30; Symphony No. 2, iii, 17–19; Chopin, Etude Op. 10 No. 11, 1–4; Haydn, "London" Symphony in D Major, i, 45–52; Mozart, Symphony No. 41 (K. 551), iii, 61–62 and 64–65; Schubert, Symphony No. 8, i, 63–68 and 85–93.

ANAPEST IN TRIPLE METER

Like dactyls, anapests arise easily in triple meter. However, where all the members of the group are equal in duration, care must be taken if the grouping is to be clear. Thus the rhythmic organization of the upper voice in the beginning of the Prelude from Bach's English Suite in G Minor (Example 68a) might have been ambiguous if taken alone—particularly when played on a harpsichord, which lacks the ability to create special stress. It is defined and specified by the anapestic groupings which enter in the lower voices. Clarity of grouping may

EXAMPLE 68

also be achieved through orchestration, as it is in the third movement (particularly measures 17 and 18) of Bach's Brandenburg Concerto No. 1 and in the first movement of Haydn's String Quartet Op. 74 No. 3 (measures 12 ff.).

The anapest is unmistakable where the upbeats are divided so that shorter note-values lead to a longer one. This is the case in the Polonaise from Handel's Concerto Grosso No. 3 in E Minor (Example 68b). Observe that the anapest grouping is supported by the accompaniment figure, except in measure 3. It is less necessary in that measure because the return to tonic harmony on the accent clearly marks the end of a group.

Harmony often plays an important role in shaping rhythm, even on low levels. A particularly clear example of this is furnished by the Minuet of Mozart's Symphony in A Major (K. 134), where the same temporal relationships are beginning-accented in the opening measures (Example 69a) and end-accented after measure 13 (Example 69b). In the first case, the harmonic-melodic motion is contained within the measure. In the second, the dominant harmony of the second and third beats moves the rhythm across the bar line to the first beat of the following measure. Note that the placement of the figure in relation to the bar line is changed because of the harmony, not the other way around.

EXAMPLE 69

For further study: Bach, Brandenburg Concerto No. 4, ii, 1–12; Beethoven, String Quartet Op. 18 No. 4, ii, 114–41; Brahms, Piano Trio Op. 101, i, 73–90; Handel, Concerto Grosso No. 1, iii, 1–4 and 18–21; Concerto Grosso No. 6, Musette, 1–4 and 18–21; Mozart, Symphony in G Major (K. 199), iv, 1–4 and 104–10; Symphony in B-flat Major (K. 319), i, 108–14; Symphony No. 39 in E-flat Major (K. 543), i, 1–8; Schumann, *Fantasiestücke*, "Grillen," 4–6.

ANAPEST IN DUPLE METER

Anapests, again like dactyls, are not commonly found in duple meter. If the three-unit group is created by subdividing one of the units, ♩ ♩ |♩ , then there is a strong tendency for the smaller values to group together, ♩ ♩ |♩ , forming an iamb with a divided upbeat. Only if the melodic-harmonic organization emphasizes each of the last two beats, will the grouping be apprehended as anapestic. The second movement of Schubert's String Quartet "Death and the Maiden" provides as unambiguous an example of this grouping as one seems likely to find (Example 70*a*).

As noted earlier, a more patent anapestic grouping can arise in duple meter

EXAMPLE 70

if the secondary accent of the measure containing the upbeat is suppressed by a syncopation. What is perhaps the classic example of this grouping is to be found in the fourth movement of Beethoven's String Quartet Op. 131 (Example 70*b*). Observe how orchestration—the alternation of the violins playing the rhythm—accompaniment and phrasing are employed to articulate this grouping.

The reason why this pattern is considered an anapest rather than a variety of inverted iamb is that the suppression of the secondary accent prevents the anacrustic group from having a focal, organizing point—from forming an independent upbeat group. The figure  , such as one finds in Example 66*b*, entering as it does on a beat, is more properly considered an iamb than an anapest. However, once again it should be observed that the rhythms are closely related in that both are clearly end-accented.

For further study: Bach, Suite No. 2 in B Minor, Rondeau, 1–2 and 32–35; Suite No. 3 in D Major, Gavotte, 1–10; Brahms, Horn Trio, i, 1–6; Haydn, String Quartet Op. 71 No. 1, i, 12–15.

AMPHIBRACH IN DUPLE AND TRIPLE METER

Amphibrach groupings are common in both duple and triple meter. The theme of the Finale of Haydn's Salomon Symphony in C Major (Example 71) is typical of the amphibrach rhythm in duple meter.

Presto assai

EXAMPLE 71

Like so many of Haydn's minuets, Example 72*a* from Symphony No. 102 in B-flat Major, is an amphibrach rhythm. In order to tie the weak afterbeat of the group to the preceding accent, there is, as has been noted, a tendency to stress the accent. In this example the stress is supplied by the turn and is intensified by the other instruments of the orchestra, which play only on the first beat of the first two measures.

Example 72*b*, from Chopin's Mazurka Op. 50 No. 2, is a somewhat more complex illustration of the amphibrach rhythm in triple meter. For in this case

a. Allegro   b. Allegretto

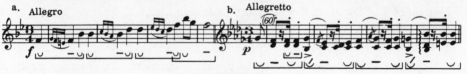

EXAMPLE 72

the accent is subdivided. This subdivision serves to tie the weak afterbeat to the accent. Notice that in this case, too, an ornament is used to stress the accent slightly. In other cases—for instance, Example 29 (p. 26)—stress is placed on the upbeat in order to make its function clear.

In the preceding examples the temporal arrangement was normal in the sense that the accent was as long as or longer than either of the weak beats. But this need not be the case. In Example 31 the anacrusis is much longer than the accent to which it moves, and it is this disproportion which gives the group its peculiar flavor. The theme of the second Bourrée of Bach's Chamber Suite No. 1 (Example 73*a*) is also a partially inverted amphibrach, the weak final beat of the group being longer than the accent. This pattern tends to close the rhythm. Indeed the closed effect is so marked that one is tempted to consider the organization to be a compound one, made up of an inverted trochee preceded by an anacrusis, as in

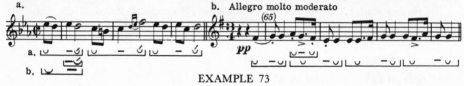

EXAMPLE 73

analysis *b*. Again the use of ornaments is of interest. The grace notes in measures 2 are important because they serve to link the weak half-note, F, to the preceding C; without them the F might well be thought of as belonging to the following accent.

Example 73*b*, from the first movement of Schubert's String Quartet in G Major (measures 64–68), is an instance of a fully inverted amphibrach—that is, the accent is the shortest note of the group. Schubert takes considerable care to make his intention clear. In measure 65 a dot is placed over the A, shortening it so that it will group with the following notes, and a stress is placed on the G in order to emphasize its anacrustic function. In the next measures the division is made clear by the motion of the accompanying voices.

For further study: Bach, Chamber Suite No. 2 in B Minor, i, 20–24; Chamber Suite No. 4 in D Major, Bourrée I, 1–8; *Well-tempered Clavier*, Vol. I, Prelude xii, 1–4; Beethoven, Piano Trio Op. 1 No. 3, iii, 1–6; String Quartet Op. 18 No. 3, iii, 16–20; Symphony No. 1, ii, 1–4; Brahms, *Variations on a Theme by Paganini*, Var. iii; Haydn, Piano Sonata No. 35 in D Major, Finale, 1–4; String Quartet Op. 71 No. 1, iv, 34–39; Mozart, Divertimento in B-flat Major (K. 270), iv, 1–4; Serenade in D Major (K. 239), iii, 54 ff.; Schumann, *Fantasiestücke*, "Ende vom Lied," 25–32.

RHYTHMIC AMBIGUITY

Rhythmic groups are not always as precisely articulated as those discussed in the preceding pages. Often they are ambiguous. There is no decisive pattern of

symbolized as A–B–A; it is A–BA. The final two periods constitute a single impulse.

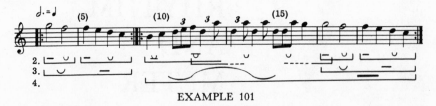

EXAMPLE 101

EXERCISES

I

A. Find two themes which are iambic and two which are anapestic on the highest architectonic levels. Find one which is trochaic and one which is dactylic on the second or third level.

B. Analyze each of these themes on all architectonic levels.

C. Write a brief essay discussing: (1) how the higher levels are created in each case— whether by pivoting, fusion, or pyramiding (try to use instances of each of these); (2) the problems encountered in the analysis of each theme.

D. How would your interpretation of the rhythmic organization affect the performance of each of these themes? Where alternative interpretations seem possible, discuss how each alternative would affect performance.

II

A. Analyze the Minuet (without trio) of Mozart's "Jupiter" Symphony and Chopin's Prelude Op. 28 No. 1. Employ the technique of rhythmic-melodic reduction where it seems useful.

B. Write a brief essay about each work, discussing such matters as the articulation of higher rhythmic levels, rhythmic inversion, rhythmic ambiguity, the influence of temporal organization on melodic structure, and so forth.

C. Choose two different recorded versions of each of these pieces. To what extent do they differ rhythmically? How does each interpretation fit with the one you have made?

III

A. Write five phrases or periods such that the highest architectonic levels exemplify each of the five rhythmic groups.

B. Write three melodies, one using a pivot, one using fusion, and one using pyramiding to unite the highest architectonic level.

C. Using the Haydn trio analyzed in this chapter as a model, write a trio of your own invention which is similar on the highest level but has a different melody and rhythmic organization on lower levels.

IV RHYTHM AND METER

The interaction of rhythm and meter is a complex one. On the one hand, the objective organization of a piece of music—the temporal relationships, melodic and harmonic structure, dynamics, and so forth—creates accents and weak beats (unaccents) and defines their relationships. And these accents and unaccents, when they occur with some regularity, would seem to specify the meter. In this sense the elements which produce rhythm also produce meter. And as we saw in connection with Examples 17, 91, and 95, changes in melodic, harmonic, and temporal relationships may result in metric changes.

On the other hand, meter can apparently be independent of rhythm, not only in the sense that it can exist in the absence of any definitive rhythmic organization, but also in the sense that rhythmic organization can conflict with and work against an established meter. Thus, for instance, beats which might become accents (potential accents) or which actually *are* accented may be at odds with the accentual scheme established in the meter. Conversely, beats which for melodic, harmonic, or other reasons would naturally be weak may be forced because of the meter to become accents. While such conflicts of natural rhythmic groups with metric structure constitute disturbances which tend to modify grouping, they need not necessarily result in a change of meter. Rather they may produce either stressed weak beats or forced accentuation.

METER AND THE BAR LINE

A word of caution seems in order here. Even in the music of the seventeenth through the nineteenth centuries time signatures and bar lines do not always accurately reflect the real metric organization. At times composers have used them somewhat casually—as a convenience—relying upon the performer to interpret and communicate the true metric structure. For instance, though the last movement of Schumann's Piano Concerto in A Minor is written in $\frac{3}{4}$ time throughout, the melody which enters at measure 80 is so strongly duple on the primary level that the time signature no longer really represents the metric structure. While the earlier triple meter continues in the minds and motor responses of the audience as well as of the performer, making the music seem somewhat strained —like a hemiole—the new meter is more like $\frac{3}{2}$ (3 × $\frac{2}{4}$) than like the previous organization of $\frac{6}{4}$ (2 × $\frac{3}{4}$). In this connection the reader should consult Example 96 (p. 81).

When we come to the interpretation and analysis of earlier music, the bar line is even less reliable as a clue to metric organization. Before the seventeenth century the bar line did not have the metric significance it later acquired. And earlier still, during the Middle Ages and the Renaissance, there were no bar lines at all. Hence the placement of the bar line in most modern editions has been determined by the editor of the work, not by the composer. Often such editors, barring the music in the light of nineteenth- and twentieth-century attitudes, have done violence to musical stylistic sense.

The use of the bar line by modern composers has not been uniform. Some composers use bar lines in the traditional way, to mark the beginning of metric units. But in much of this music the metric crossing of voices is such a common occurrence that while the bar line will indicate the meter of one voice, it will not do so for another. Indeed, composers have written the meters of different voices with different time signatures (as Bartók does in his String Quartet No. 3, measures 370–80), made the beams of series of eighth- or sixteenth-notes run across bar lines, and used many other notational devices to indicate something about the metric structure. Other composers seem currently to be using the bar line to mark off the limits of melodic, harmonic, or rhythmic groups rather than to designate the beginning of metric units. In general the bar line has become less and less indicative of metric organization. And it must not be considered conclusive evidence of the metric scheme.

NON-CONGRUENCE

LATENT METER AND RHYTHMIC STRUCTURE

Sometimes the particular organization of a theme or passage makes two different interpretations of the metric structure possible. One cannot be certain at first whether, for instance, the meter is duple or triple, though once a decision is made (perhaps on the basis of subsequent developments), the resulting metric structuring will be neither vague nor ambiguous.

Such an equivocal melodic-rhythmic organization is presented by the opening theme of the second movement of Mozart's "Jupiter" Symphony. The theme might have been written in duple meter, as shown in Example 102. This looks convincing. The opening beat functions well as an upbeat, the stressed offbeats come in the right place, and so on. And although the meter becomes manifestly triple in the following measures (see Example 103), the theme could conceivably have been written in duple meter throughout. Certainly a *latent* duple meter is very strong in these first measures.

However, the melody is, as Mozart makes clear (Example 103), definitely in triple, *not* in duple meter. Nor should the theme be thought of or played as metrically ambiguous or vague. There are two reasons for this. From a historical point of view, the rhythm is that of a sarabande, with its typically heavy second beat (see Example 51*a*, p. 40). Since this rhythm is normally precise, it would be stylistically wrong to perform it ambiguously. From the point of view of internal structure, too, the triple meter should be decisively articulated. For if the latent duple organization is permitted to obscure or dominate the manifest

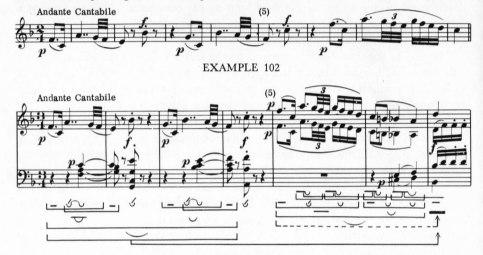

EXAMPLE 102

EXAMPLE 103

triple meter, the meaning and character, not only of the theme itself but of the whole movement as developing out of the theme, are considerably weakened.

As is often the case, the rhythmic organization of this passage can be better understood if its melodic structure is made clear. The theme establishes three separable, though interrelated, strands of melodic motion. These are labeled *a*, *b*, and *c* in the analysis given in Example 104. The most important of these strands—the one that leads the ear most forcefully—is clearly strand *a*, which moves up stepwise from A to B-flat to C to D. Mozart emphasizes the importance of this line with a supporting accompaniment, labeled *a'*, which moves in tenths with it. But as indicated in Example 104, as well as in the rhythmic analysis given in Example 103, these vital melodic tones are not accents. They are stressed weak beats which seek to become accents. And the sense of restrained tension which the melody communicates is the result of the fact that potential accents are forced to act as weak beats. They constitute an urgent anacrusis and their potential is realized in the heavily accented D, in which is released the cumulative potential of the earlier tones. Coming, as it does, on the first really satisfactory downbeat thus far, the D would have been accented even had it been marked "piano" (cf. Example 137, measure 280).

All this is lost if the theme is thought of and performed in a dominantly duple meter. For the A in measure 1 is then an accented goal—a point of stability— rather than a tone imbued with the necessity for motion. So too are the B-flat in measure 3 and the C in measure 6. And the importance of the D is so minimized that it almost constitutes an anticlimax.

Measures 5 and 6 have not yet been discussed. Melodically they perform two functions. At first they act to complete and fill in most of the structural gaps created in the earlier measures. And at the end they make manifest an intervallic

EXAMPLE 104

motion present, but hidden, in the earlier measures. That is, the unheard interval of a fourth from F (measure 1) to B-flat (measure 2) in the first group and from G to C in the second group is continued and made patent to the ear in the skip from A to D (measures 6–7).

Metrically measures 5 and 6 are less decisive in feeling than the earlier measures. They constitute a continuous and progressive anacrusis to the accented D— that is, each group seems to be an upbeat to the next, as the accented part of a beat becomes weak. This effect occurs partly because each group is faster than the one which follows. In order to insure this feeling of progressive anacruses, care must be taken in performance not to stress the C in measure 6 but rather to make the two eighth-notes move smoothly, as an anacrusis, into the two quarter-notes, which are themselves anacrustic to the D.

In short, measures 5 and 6 are a proximate anacrusis to measures 7 through 10—a kind of parenthetical upbeat—while measures 1 through 4 are the *real*, though remote, anacrusis to the second part of the theme, which begins on the accented D. This is not mere speculation. Mozart makes the anacrustic character of the first four measures clear in the coda (measures 92 ff.), where the par- enthetical anacrusis is omitted and the real anacrusis, the basic melodic strand A–B-flat–C, moves directly to the D.

It should be clear from this analysis how the latent duple meter, placing considerable stress upon weak beats, shapes the sense and character of the theme. But as was observed earlier, the latent duple organization of the theme also has important consequences later in the movement. Under its influence, so to speak, duple meter continually breaks through the basic triple meter of the movement. It is manifest, for example, in the bridge passage (measures 23–25), in the second half of the subordinate theme (measures 32–37), in the development section (measures 51–59), and in the recapitulation (measures 67–70 and measures 80–86). Each of these passages is an instance of a clear duple meter written within a ¾ bar scheme. To illustrate, the second half of the subordinate theme is given in Example 105.

EXAMPLE 105

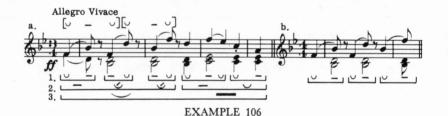

EXAMPLE 106

FORCED ACCENTUATION AND RHYTHMIC STRUCTURE

In the Mozart theme just discussed, tones which might have been (one is tempted to say "should have been") accented are constrained to act as weak beats. In the Scherzo of Beethoven's Symphony No. 4 (Example 106*a*), the reverse of this takes place—that is, a tone which should have been a weak beat is forced into being accented.

It might at first glance seem that the tension of the first two measures arises because the triple meter of the melody conflicts with the duple meter of the accompaniment. But this is not the basis for tension. The melody could without any difficulty have been heard as duple (Example 106*b*). Indeed, Beethoven himself uses almost the same melody in duple meter in the final movement of his Symphony No. 5 (measures 319 ff.).

The strained striving of these first measures is rather the result of the duple accompaniment being so placed that potentially weak beats are forced to become accents. Thus if the theme were heard in duple meter, it would naturally fall into three end-accented groups. We would want to accent the note which follows the skip. This normal group is in fact established by the opening iamb, which seems quite relaxed. And had the accompaniment coincided with the iambic groups, as in Example 106b, the result would have been very ordinary. On the other hand, considered in triple meter, without the conflicting accompaniment, the tune would easily fall into freely moving amphibrachs, as indicated by the brackets above the example. It is of some moment to realize that the tune is potentially amphibrach, because this enables one to understand the tremendous feeling of freedom and release which measure 3 creates, where the suppressed amphibrach breaks through.

The analysis given below Example 106a indicates (and Beethoven corroborates this with his rests and phrasing) that the meter of the accompaniment is to be taken seriously; it must dominate the natural meter of the melodic line. The second and third groups are to be performed as trochees on the primary level. Notice how important it is to hear and perform the first group as an iamb. For only then do the power of the rhythmic reversal from iamb to trochee and the strained accentuation make themselves forcefully felt. If the first group is heard as a trochee or if later groups are allowed to relax into a swinging triple meter, the whole effect is weakened.

The instability of this uncomfortable conflict between the natural accentuation of the melody and the metric accents of the accompaniment (harmony is constant) makes the trochees act as stressed weak beats on the second architectonic level. And the whole dactylic group (level 2), striving for stability, acts as an anacrusis to the second half of the phrase.

The function of the conflict between meter and melody thus becomes clear. It creates the strident, striving character of the theme and at the same time welds the whole phrase into a single dynamic impulse toward a goal. Without the conflict, the resulting amphibrachs would have been pleasantly dancelike at best, and the character of the impulse on the third architectonic level would have been much less forceful and cohesive.

Although not always as striking as in Examples 103 and 106a, instances of non-congruence between meter and melody are quite common in music literature. For instance, the rhythmic organization of the opening of the Scherzo of the "Eroica" Symphony (Example 88) also depends, as we have seen, upon the presence of a changing-note figure which tends to be duple in a metric scheme which is definitely triple.

STABLE METER AND SHIFTING GROUPS

But non-congruence does not invariably produce stressed weak beats and forcefully directed anacruses. It may, at times, cause a rhythmic organization which would otherwise have been regular and stable to fluctuate. Non-congruence produces this sort of irregularity in a passage in the first movement of Bruckner's Symphony No. 9 (Example 107*a*). The excerpt occurs twenty-six measures after letter *T* in the Eulenburg miniature score.

The tonal-temporal organization of this passage does not create an unequivocal rhythmic-melodic shape. Although the motivic repetition makes it clear that the melodic grouping is in fours, the sequence is so uniform that any one of the notes could constitute the beginning of a regular and continuous pattern (see Example 107*b*). The inherent ambiguity of the tonal-temporal organization is empha-

EXAMPLE 107

sized by the counterpoint in the lower strings, which play the same pattern against that of the first violins, that is, beginning at a different point. Notice, incidentally, that in the actual passage (Example 107*a*) the triplets do in fact place accents so that each of the patterns in Example 107*b* is brought out. That is, the first metric accent (counting in threes) marks the beginning of pattern 1, the second metric accent marks the beginning of pattern 4, and so forth. Because of the melodic ambiguity and above all because there is no temporal differentiation to define an unequivocal pattern of accents and weak beats, a triple meter is able to impose itself upon the weakly duple melodic organization.

However, though the meter is able to impose its accentual scheme upon the melody, the melodic group still maintains its identity as a pattern. That is, the meter determines the placement of the accents and weak beats within the pattern, but does not make the four-note unit into a three-note one. Since the mind tends to perceive an organization in the simplest way possible, it is easier for the mind to maintain the four-note melodic pattern and change its point of accentuation than to keep changing the structure of each successive melodic group (and perhaps its rhythm as well), which would be the case if meter determined melodic organization.

It was observed earlier that the melodic sequence is such that several different patterns, each of which is regular, might arise. But it must be added that one sequence may create a more forcefully structured pattern, more patent to the ear, than another. In this otherwise uniform pattern there is one obvious point of articulation—the skip of a third—which serves to differentiate and separate the groups. As a result, the clearest and most natural way to group these tones is that of the descending scale.

Thus while metric structure determines the placement of the accent within groups, melodic structure orders the length and organization of the groups. However, because the melodic repetition in fours is not congruent with the metric recurrence in threes, the position of the accent within the melodic pattern keeps changing. The result, as can be seen from the analysis given in Example

EXAMPLE 108

108, is a continual shifting of both the structure and proportions of the rhythmic groups.

As the reader listens to this passage, he will observe that the irregularity of the rhythm can be maintained (in the last four groups) despite the fact that it is, as Bruckner indicates, to be played "more and more legato." This is possible for two reasons. First, because the same pitches are repeated, we are more aware of their changing function in the rhythm. Take the tone E, for instance. At first it is a weak afterbeat in a dactyl group (see * in Example 108), which itself acts as an upbeat to the next measure; then the E becomes an anacrusis, and finally it acts as an accent. Or looked at the other way around: on the lowest architectonic level each accent in the final measures occurs on a different pitch—first F, then C-sharp, then D, and lastly E. In earlier measures, however, tones tended to maintain their functions because the melodic groups themselves moved in pitch. Thus in measures 27 and 28 (see Example 107) the F is the only accented note.

Second, group differentiation is more marked in measures 29 and 30 than in earlier ones because the first note (F) of later groups does not belong to the same harmony as the final note (C-sharp) of the preceding group. Up to these last four groups, the final note of one scale and the first note of the next could be

understood as belonging to the same harmony, thus making the transition between groups smooth and less marked.

This ease of transition from group to group makes the latent dactylic rhythm,
which pure meter would impose, quite strong in the first two measures and in the
similar measures which precede this excerpt in the movement. And insofar as
such dactylic groups influence our perception of this passage, they would, as
noted earlier, tend to make melodic structure seem irregular.

There is then a danger of oversimplification. Actually, until the final measures
of this passage we are aware—though not perhaps consciously—of both these
modes of organization. Both play a part in our experience and both must be ac-
counted for in our analysis.

This discussion points to an important fact, namely, that meter is not simply a
matter of regularly recurring dynamic intensification. It is a set of proportional
relationships, an ordering framework of accents and weak beats within which
rhythmic grouping takes place. It constitutes the matrix out of which rhythm
arises.

Thus the rhythm and hence the meaning of the passage (Example 108) would
have been very different had Bruckner written it in fours with a stress on every
third beat (Example 109).

EXAMPLE 109

Which comes first, the chicken or the egg? Does rhythm determine meter, or
is it the other way around? The answer depends upon the point from which the
process is viewed. For the composer, the rhythmic-melodic organization to be
projected determines the meter chosen. For the performer, the meter indicated
by the composer limits, though it does not in and of itself determine, the possibilities of grouping. For both composer and performer—as well as for the listener
—meter establishes a structured continuum of accents and weak beats which
acts as a basis for rhythmic and melodic expectation; that is, it becomes a norm
in the light of which both the regular and irregular are apprehended and felt.

It has from time to time been emphasized that stress on a weak beat does not
make the beat into an accent and that, for this reason, even regularly recurring
stresses will not change a given metric organization. And as long as melodic
articulation, temporal differentiation, and so forth are such that strongly shaped
patterns are created, this rule holds. But when melodic shapes are ambiguous
and temporal differentiation is absent, strongly stressed weak beats may under-

mine the existing meter, making the metric organization seem uncertain. The stressed offbeats in Example 109, for instance, create a sense of metric insecurity. Where there is no melodic, temporal, or other differentiation at all, offbeat stresses tend, when they are regular, to determine the meter and, when they are irregular, to destroy all sense of meter (see Example 111).

SHIFTING METER AND STABLE GROUPS

In general, the more uniform and *un*organized (not disorganized) a passage is, the more susceptible it is to outside influences—to melodic or temporal patterns in other parts of the musical texture, and to stress. Indeed in the absence of any objective basis for metric organization, the mind will tend to impose its own meter upon the series of undifferentiated pulses.

Whether such subjective groupings are determined by the nature of human mental processes or whether they arise out of the listener's stylistic habits and

EXAMPLE 110

dispositions is a question which requires further study. Probably both play a part. But whatever the reason, it appears that in our culture, at least for the past few centuries, such a series of pulses tends to be mentally organized into a duple meter. Any fair sampling of the metric organizations used in Western music will show a clear preponderance of duple over triple organization. For while meter is frequently triple on lower metric levels, it is seldom so on higher ones, as an examination of the examples in this book will show.

Thus when the ear is presented with a series of pulses such as one finds at the beginning of the second movement of Beethoven's Symphony No. 8, it tends to organize the beats into two four-pulse units (Example 110). And when the melody enters, this subjective organization is confirmed. (Of course the conductor with prior knowledge of Beethoven's notation and of the subsequent melodic and rhythmic organization may project this grouping in performance. But such an objective articulation does not seem desirable here. The series should be played uniformly.)

It might at first appear that the rhythm of the melody is against the meter—that is, as indicated by the brackets over the example, that the rhythm consists of an anapest with the dotted eighth-note, F, as the accent. This is plausible because the temporal organization would seem to be short–short–long. However, if the melodic-temporal relationships are considered more carefully and are reduced to their essentials, it is clear that the eighth-note F is not a goal. There has been no melodic or harmonic movement toward it. (This analysis is supported by the fact that at measure 9 [see score], where the same temporal distribution is imbued with a clearly directed melodic motion from B-flat up to E-flat, Beethoven is careful to prevent the goal of the motion—the E-flat—from becoming an accent by introducing syncopation.) The rhythm is in fact a trochee with a divided accent: ⌣⌣⌣ ⌣ . The subjective organization imposed by the mind of the listener on the opening measure serves to support this organization by making the meter begin on the first pulse of the measure.

Although the partial phrase in the cellos corresponds with the opening meter, when it stops in the middle of measure 4 the wind accompaniment like that which began the movement establishes a new placement of the meter in relation to the bar lines. Both the meter of the pulse accompaniment and that of the theme now begin on the second half of the measure, ignoring the bar lines. The original, "correct" placement of the meter is resumed, after another partial phrase, in measure 8.

THE INFLUENCE OF STRESS UPON METER

The beginning of the "Dances of the Adolescents" from Stravinsky's *The Rite of Spring* provides an interesting instance of the influence of stress upon a series of pulses (Example 111).

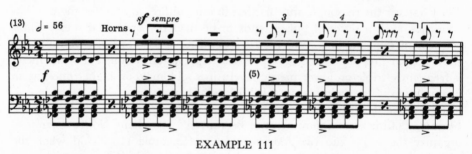

EXAMPLE 111

At the outset, the metric organization, whether imposed by the mind of the listener or by the articulation of the orchestra, is clearly in duple meter. Nor is this impression weakened by the stressed offbeats in measure 3. Instead, these stresses, coming as dynamic intensifications most frequently do, confirm our sense of duple meter. They are felt as regular offbeats, and had they continued in measure 5, the meter would not have been weakened one whit.

The metric organization begins to seem insecure with the stress on the first beat of measure 6. This happens for two reasons. (1) Because special stress seems appropriate to and has thus far occurred only on weak beats, the stressed accent feels misplaced—wrong. It is as though the accent were not really an accent but a weak beat. (2) The number of pulses from accent to accent is no longer regular and normal for a duple meter. That is, instead of stresses being separated by two or four pulses which would fit the meter, the stress on the first beat of measure 6 occurs after three pulses. And because the recurrence of stress continues to be irregular—coming after three pulses, then four, and finally five (see brackets above Example 111)—our sense of metric organization is almost completely destroyed.

SYNCOPATIONS, SUSPENSIONS, AND TIES

DEFINITIONS

The passage from *The Rite of Spring* raises an important question of definition and terminology. Such stressed weak beats are often referred to as "syncopations." But there is a vast difference between the rhythmic and metric organization of Example 111 and the organization which results if the same chords are played with the following temporal relationships:

In this version the sense of meter is *not* weakened. Rather, by suppressing the downbeats, the ties create strong anacruses to measures 5, 6, and 9, and make the first beats of those measures strongly accented. Since the rhythmic-metric organization and the effect of these two versions are so very different, it would seem that only confusion can result from calling both stressed weak beats and ties "syncopations."

Let us take another instance. Both the *Harvard Dictionary of Music*[1] and *Grove's Dictionary of Music and Musicians*[2] cite the opening measures of the third movement of Brahms's Symphony No. 4 as an example of syncopation. However, though the phrasing creates stressed weak beats which modify the groupings on the lowest level, making them end-accented (Example 112a) rather than beginning-accented (Example 112b), this is very different from the effect and the rhythmic organization created by genuine syncopation (Example 112c).

How then shall syncopation be defined? As employed in this book, the term

[1] Willi Apel, *op. cit.*, p. 726.
[2] (3d ed.; New York: Macmillan Co., 1936), V, 242.

"syncopation" refers to a tone which enters where there is no pulse on the primary metric level (the level on which beats are counted and felt) and where the following beat on the primary metric level is either absent (a rest) or suppressed (tied). It follows from this that whether there is syncopation or not depends upon how the beat or pulse continuum is felt and hence upon the tempo of the piece as well as upon the performer's articulation of the meter. If the tempo is too slow or if the performer overarticulates lower metric levels, the effect of syncopated notes may be weakened. Or if the tempo is too fast, what should be a higher metric level is felt to be the primary metric level, and notes not intended to be syncopated become so.

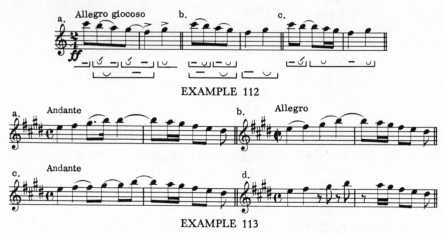

EXAMPLE 112

EXAMPLE 113

Thus the B in the opening motive from the aria "Ev'ry Valley" from Handel's *Messiah* (Example 113a) is *not* syncopated because at the andante tempo it comes on a pulse, albeit a weak one. However, the variants which follow *are* syncopated. In the first of these the time is cut and the tempo faster and because we count the measure in twos rather than in fours, the B does not come on a beat—even a weak one. In variants c and c' both the G-sharp and the B are syncopated.

The importance of the suppression of the downbeat B in the second measure of the variants is obvious. As the reader can test for himself, if the B is sounded or heard as a separate impulse, there is no effect of syncopation. If we now turn back to Example 111, we must revise our analysis somewhat. While the strings playing continuous pulses are not syncopated, the horns, which play only offbeats, are syncopated (see also Beethoven, *Grosse Fuge*, Examples 156–58, pp. 164–66).

If the note B in Example 113a is not a syncopation, what is it? Unfortunately we have no unambiguous term for this. However, rather than introduce a new term we shall broaden the use of the term "suspension" to include tones which enter on a weak pulse and are held over, even if they do not become literally dissonant. For not only are such tones similar to harmonically activated suspensions in their general configuration and placement within the metric scheme, but because they are tied from a weak pulse they are imbued with a strong need to move and hence feel like and act like those suspensions which actually become dissonant.

Suspensions must be distinguished from *ties*. A "tie," as the term will be used here, denotes a tone which enters on an accent rather than on a weak beat.

This means that the word "suspension" will be used in two senses. First, it will designate a tied note which enters on a weak beat. As is the case in Example 113*a*, this note need not become a dissonance. Second, it denotes a tied note which actually becomes a dissonance. Thus in Example 114, excerpts from the same aria in *Messiah* are used to illustrate: (*a*) a suspension which does not become dissonant, (*b*) a suspension which does become dissonant, (*c*) a simple tie, and (*d*) a tie which becomes a suspension (dissonance) in the second sense of the term.

EXAMPLE 114

Thus the difference between a tie, a suspension, and a syncopation lies in their placement in relation to metric pulses. A tie comes on a strong beat within the meter. In a compound meter it enters at the beginning of either half of the measure: in $\frac{4}{4}$ time, it may begin on either the first beat or the third; in $\frac{6}{8}$ time on either the first pulse or the fourth; and so forth. A suspension begins on a weak pulse within the metric scheme. A syncopation begins where there is no beat on the primary metric level.

STRESS AND SYNCOPATION

One of the things which all musicians will have noticed is that there is a marked tendency to perceive or perform syncopated notes as emphasized even though such emphasis is not marked by he composer.[3] Perhaps this is intuitively done to compensate for the fact that there is no pulse at that point—to give the note a "beat status" which it does not really have. In any case, because emphasis and syncopation seem to belong together in this way, it is possible to make a suspension feel like a syncopation by adding stress to it. Thus if the B in Example 113*a* or the E in Example 114*a* are stressed, they will feel like syncopations.

These observations call attention to a function of stress not yet considered, namely, that it may be used not to change grouping but to modify the character of a rhythmic group. It is this function of stress which Schumann exploits in the Scherzo of his Symphony No. 4 (Example 115).

The inverted amphibrach and inverted trochees in measures 8–14 are not syncopations. No pulse is missing or suppressed. Since the tempo is fast, the primary metric level moves in dotted half-notes, and hence the weak part of the trochee *is* followed by a pulse. The function of the stress is to make this part of the group feel like a syncopation even though it is not one.

EXAMPLE 115

Actually in this case the fact that the stress comes on an inverted group gives it such power that the rhythmic-metric scheme is almost upset; the stress hovers on the brink of becoming an accent. As a consequence of this, the G-sharp in measure 15 seems strained. If the metric placement were changed so that the half-notes became accents and the eighth-notes became upbeats, making the rhythm iambic, then the G-sharp would itself become a syncopation. And though this does not take place, it comes so close to happening that we feel the tension anyhow.

SYNCOPATION AND MELODIC-RHYTHMIC STRUCTURE

Although the role of syncopation is sometimes primarily that of characterizing a theme or a passage, more often it performs a crucial function in shaping the whole pattern of musical progress. And this is precisely what it does in the first period of the Minuet of Mozart's Symphony in G Minor (K. 550; Example 116).

The initial group is three measures long. The primary metric level is that of the measure. On the lowest rhythmic level the accent which should arrive at the

[3] See H. E. Weaver, "Syncopation: A Study in Musical Rhythms," *Journal of General Psychology*, XX (1939), 409–29.

beginning of measure 2 is suppressed and the rhythm is fused together by the syncopation across the bar. The suppression of this accent makes all the beats, beginning with the B-flat in measure 1, anacrustic to the last G of the group and its afterbeat, D. However, the first G is also accented, and one may ask why the whole group is not a trochee or even perhaps a dactyl. In order to understand the structure and behavior of this group, it is necessary to analyze the melodic and harmonic structure of the phrase as well as its temporal organization.

Whenever an accent is suppressed, as it is in this case, the mind, searching for the focal stability of an accent with reference to which it can group weak beats, places particularly stress on the subsequent downbeat. Furthermore, the stronger the potential of the unrealized accent—the stronger it would have been had it not been suppressed—the more effective the syncopation and the more forceful the impulse toward the next accent.

EXAMPLE 116

EXAMPLE 117

In this case the suppressed beat is crucial because had it been presented it would have organized not only the primary architectonic level but the second and third levels as well. If the melodic-rhythmic organization had been allowed to follow its initial impulse, it would have continued upward through the triad to an accented high D, which would be a natural point for the completion of the upward thrust begun in the first measure. This is shown by the motion of the oboes and clarinets, which move through the G minor triad in just this way and by the motion of all the other instruments to D at the beginning of measure 2.

Had the melody reached an accented high D, the rhythm of the initial two-measure unit would have been iambic and that of the phrase might have been trochaic. The missing D is therefore the tone which would have been accented on all levels. This can perhaps be more clearly seen if the Minuet from Schubert's Symphony No. 5 in B-flat is considered along with the Mozart Minuet. For the Schubert Minuet begins exactly like the Mozart one but continues in a much more normal and regular way (Example 117).

Here the melodic motion begun in measure 1 reaches its goal on the high D immediately, and the second iamb is accented. This accent in turn contributes to the organization of the second and third architectonic levels.

Thus what is suppressed in the Mozart is not simply a lower architectonic accent but the beat which might have been the focal point for the organization of the total structure. This has several consequences. (1) It places an unusually heavy stress upon the weak beat, B-flat; the performer feels the interruption strongly and compensates for it by emphasizing the B-flat. (2) It makes the following accent on G so powerful and the whole shape so end-accented that the motion of this impulse is brought to an unequivocal halt. (3) It shapes the progress of the subsequent melodic motion, for the denial of the expected D makes the need for it even greater. In a sense the whole theme is a search for a D which comes on a strongly accented beat—and this tone is not forthcoming until the final note of the melody (see Example 118).

EXAMPLE 118

Lastly, in discussing the anacrustic character of this group, one should not neglect the importance of the harmony in articulating the rhythm. The weight and tendency of the B-flat toward the G are considerably increased by the fact that it is treated as part of a $^{6-5}_{4-3}$ progression leading to the tonic chord.

The second phrase (measures 4–6) is constructed in the same way as the first. Here another difference between the Schubert and the Mozart Minuets is apparent. Because Schubert's two phrases are in the relation of antecedent to consequent, they establish a completed rhythmic unit. This is not the case with the Mozart Minuet. Here the phrases are harmonically as well as rhythmically parallel. As a result, once the second group is begun, both are heard as upbeats to some expected longer group which will constitute an accent.

Though melodically the new phrase (Example 118) begins like the first one, it is clearly set off harmonically from what has gone before. For it moves away from the earlier tonic harmony and is harmonized with an E-flat triad, which functions as the Neapolitan second in D minor.

The end of the syncopated group now becomes the basis for a descending sequence. It is as though the pent-up energy of the two initial accents in measures 3 and 6 had been released. However, although the impulse created by this new syncopation still places a stress upon the accent which follows it, the force carried over is no longer concentrated on a single accent but is distributed—even dissipated—over three similarly placed accents. And as the passage unfolds, the equality of the parts of the sequential series makes even the group ending on F seem weak in retrospect. In other words, though each anapest in the series is clearly shaped and differentiated, the groups themselves are so equal that none is able to serve as the focal accent around which the units themselves can be grouped. What is needed is a clearly organized accented group to which this sequence can be related.

The necessity for such a group and the importance of its particular organization can perhaps best be illustrated by writing several alternative endings for this theme. Part *a* of Example 119 is unsatisfactory for several reasons. First, by

EXAMPLE 119

simply continuing the series, it ends on a very weak group—though the listener will probably do his best to make the ending seem strong. Second, the melody now ends on the tonic. This melodic step has already received much emphasis and now constitutes a feeble anticlimax. But, even more important, the end is weak harmonically. For this phrase, having moved away from the tonic harmony to a tonal area around D, now simply collapses back to where it started from without any real tonal departure. Third, as we have seen, the first part of the theme sets up the tone D as an important goal. And part *a* of the example leaves this motion unfulfilled. Finally, and perhaps most important of all, the final phrase is now regular relative to the preceding ones: the structure of the theme as a whole is 3–3–6. After the strained, compact structures of the two earlier groups such flaccid regularity is a vapid anticlimax.

It is this regularity of phrase structure which constitutes the major flaw in parts *b* and *c* of this example. Only by stretching the length—by weakening the intermediate accents for the sake of the final one—can the tension of the final groups make them an adequate culmination of the earlier ones. This is accomplished after the octave transfer by extending the downward motion of the scale passage still further (see Example 118, measures 11–12), and just at this point the melodic motion becomes more uniform, moving chromatically rather than diatonically down from the B-flat. The melodic ambiguity thus created is reflected in the constant dovetailing and pivoting of rhythmic groups. Thus the return to clarity in measure 13 is indeed impressive. And the accent, arising from a return to melodic, harmonic, and rhythmic certainty after the suspense and doubts of the preceding measures, is strong enough to carry the burden of the previous intensity and to bring the whole theme to a satisfactory conclusion.

METRIC CROSSING

As we noted earlier, the meter of a piece of music—the way it is barred—indicates and limits, though it does not necessarily specify, the possibilities of rhythmic organization. Of course when a composition is in a familiar style whose musical norms have become part of our habit responses, barring does not seem of crucial importance. Like punctuation in literature, it is felt to facilitate grouping but not to determine it. Stylistic experience would in most cases enable musicians to reconstruct the rhythmic-metric organization, even if bar lines were missing.

But if the norms of a style are in doubt or if the temporal-melodic organization is such that several groupings seem equally possible, then the absence of a specified meter may create problems of interpretation whose solution will play an important role in determining rhythmic organization. Suppose, for instance, that we were asked to perform the melody in Example 120a. In order to do so it would be necessary to decide how it is to be grouped—where the accents and weak beats come. We would have to decide what the meter is.

EXAMPLE 120

One possible solution would be to interpret the rhythm as a series of amphibrachs, in which case the meter would be in $\frac{3}{4}$ time, as shown in Example 120b. However, since this melody is accompanied by a counterpoint in other instruments, we know that this is not the correct placement for the meter. As indicated in Example 121, the rhythmic group begins on an accent, not on an upbeat. As it stands here, it appears that the melody is syncopated within the bar against the regular meter of the accompaniment. As a result, the syncopated beats act as upbeats to the following accent. Notice that this produces a polyrhythm—the melody is end-accented and the accompaniment is beginning-accented—but not a polymeter. Both parts are in $\frac{3}{4}$.

Fortunately in this case the composer put in bar lines to tell us what rhythmic organization he intended. The excerpt is a somewhat simplified version of measures 3–11 from the third movement of Bartók's Piano Concerto No. 3. As is clear from Example 122, Bartók intended no syncopation. The upper voice is barred in ⅜ meter, and the rhythm of the upper part is trochaic on the lowest architectonic level.

Both the trochees comprising the two-measure group are "abnormal." The first (♪♪) is inverted and the second (♩ ♪), because of temporal differentiation, "wants" to become end-accented. There is a tendency, that is, for the weak final eighth-note to become an upbeat to the following measure. To prevent this from happening, the preceding accent must be somewhat stressed.

EXAMPLE 121

EXAMPLE 122*

Our understanding of the rhythm of the upper voice depends in part upon the counterpoint of the lower voice, which also influences our apprehension of the whole texture. The lower voice is in triple meter (3 × ⅜). This is made very clear by the repetition of the pattern. The grouping is beginning-accented. This is a product not only of the instrumental stress placed on the first beat of the group by the whole orchestra but also of the dynamic stress on the second beat. The latter stress prevents the final quarter-note of the group from becoming an upbeat. Observe that by writing the eighth-note beams across the bar lines,

♩ ♫ ♩ , Bartók makes it clear that this is not a syncopation. Had he written

♩ ♪|♪♩ , the lower part might have been thought of as syncopated and the stresses would have had a different meaning.

Because our minds tend to organize the musical texture in the simplest way, simultaneous musical events will, if possible, be apprehended as having one basic mode of articulation. It is for this reason that the beginning-accented grouping of the lower part is able to impose its organization upon the upper part, so that the upper group also ends after the second measure. Thus the upper part becomes trochaic on the second level.

The articulation into two-measure units is also a result of the crossing of the upper meter, which is $2 \times$ ⅜, with the lower meter, which is $3 \times$ ²⁄₈. This creates what Curt Sachs has called a metric "dissonance"[4] (D) at the beginning of measure 2 which is resolved to a "consonance" (C) on the first beat of measure 3: ♩♩ ♩♩ ♩♩|♩ . This crossing groups the smaller units, the trochees of the upper voice, and separates larger ones, by determining the primary metric level. That is, it forces us to feel the basic meter moving from one metric consonance to another in two-measure units.

Not only does the lower part give rise to this two-measure unit, but it also articulates the structure of the phrase as a whole. Because the groups in the upper part are more or less similar in length and structure, they do not create unambiguous groups on higher architectonic levels. However, the final groups of the lower part are linked by a rhythmic pivot (see analysis under Example 122). As a result the whole period, including the upper part, is apprehended as a well-structured anapest.

The problems posed in the preceding discussion of the theme of the last movement of Bartók's Piano Concerto No. 3 were fictitious, first, in the sense that the composer had in fact written bar lines specifying the metric organization and, second, in the sense that we know from stylistic experience—hearing and experiencing this kind of music—how this passage should sound.

But these problems are not fictitious when we turn to music of the Middle Ages and the Renaissance. Composers then used no bar lines, and we are not at all sure what the norms of the style really are—how this music was performed and how it sounded.

Since analysis of the rhythmic-metric organization of late medieval and Renaissance music has only recently begun,[5] what follows must be considered tentative rather than definitive. However, in spite of its provisional nature, an

---

[4] *Rhythm and Tempo* (New York: W. W. Norton, 1953), p. 41.

[5] See Otto Gombosi, "Machaut's *Messe Notre-Dame*," *Musical Quarterly*, XXXVI (1950), 204–24; see also his reviews in the *Journal of the American Musicological Society*, IV (1951), 139–47; VI (1953), 240–43; VII (1954), 221–28. And W. Scott Goldthwaite, "Rhythmic Patterns and Formal Symmetry in the 15th Century Chanson" (Ph.D. diss., Harvard University, 1955).

exploratory investigation is of value. In the first place, this music involves rhythmic-metric procedures rather different from those we have discussed thus far: ones in which meter is more than the matrix out of which rhythm arises. For as Gombosi and Goldthwaite have shown, metric relationships both within and between voices are a fundamental shaping force in this music. Indeed in the work to be analyzed metric alternation and metric crossing are a basic facet of compositional technique. In the second place, as will become very apparent, a discussion of this music of necessity emphasizes the ultimate dependence of interpretation and performance, as well as analysis, upon stylistic understanding.

EXAMPLE 123

The work chosen to illustrate these matters is the Kyrie from Dufay's *Missa Sancti Jacobi* (Example 123). The text is that given in Arnold Schering's *Geschichte der Musik in Beispielen*.[6] Schering's note-values, however, have been halved in order to make the metric problems more patent as well as to make the notation conform more closely to present-day practice.

Let us look first at the tenor, since this voice, taken from plainsong, generally served as the point of departure for the composer. It is divided into two large

[6] (Leipzig: Breitkopf und Härtel, 1931), pp. 33–34.

sections (labeled A and B), each of which is in turn divided into two parts (indicated by long brackets below). The second part of each section has the same temporal arrangement as the first part.

Sections A and B differ from each other not only melodically but also metrically. Section A, consisting of two four-measure phrases, is in duple meter on the highest level; Section B, consisting of two three-measure phrases, is triple on the highest level. Observe that as one moves from higher to lower levels, the metric organization changes. Thus in the first section the tenor is duple $(2 \times \frac{3}{4})$ on the highest level, in the next lower level it is triple $(3 \times \frac{1}{4})$; and the lowest level, again duple $(2 \times \frac{1}{8})$. In Section B the order is triple–duple–triple. The two metric hierarchies look like this:

Section A   Section B

1. ⌊𝅗𝅥·   𝅗𝅥·⌋ (2 x 3/4)   ⌊𝅗𝅥·   𝅗𝅥·   𝅗𝅥·⌋ (3 x 6/8)

i. ⌊♩♩♩♩♩♩⌋ (3 x 2/8)   ⌊𝅗𝅥· 𝅗𝅥· 𝅗𝅥· 𝅗𝅥·𝅗𝅥· 𝅗𝅥·⌋ (2 x 3/8)

ii. ⌊♫♫♫⌋ etc. (2 x 1/8)   ⌊♫♫♫⌋ etc. (3 x 1/8)

Turning now to the cantus and the countertenor, we find that although the highest metric level (labeled 1, above) in Section A is clearly duple (two-measure units), the organization of level i, and consequently of level ii as well, is less certain. For instance, the cantus in measure 3 might be thought of as being either duple, ♩♩♩♪♩ (3 + 3) , or triple, ♩♩♫♩ (2 + 2 + 2) ; similarly, measure 7 might be interpreted as a syncopated triple meter, ♩♩♫♩ (2 + 2 + 2) , or as a compound (duple) meter, ⌊♪♩ ♩♪⌋ (3 + 3) . Measures 3 and 5 in the countertenor are even more open to different metric interpretations: each could be either triple, ♩ ♩♩♩ (2 + 2 + 2) , or duple, ⌊♩ ♪♪♩⌋ (3 + 3) .

The choices made between these alternatives are no minor matter. They will affect not only the rhythmic groupings of the cantus part but will also determine the interrelationships between the voices and ultimately the structure and meaning of the Kyrie as a whole.

On what basis can such decisions be made? Were the style a familiar one with a living tradition of performance—one whose norms had become part of our habit responses—there would be no problem. For instance, had these temporal relationships occurred in a piece by Haydn or Mozart, they would almost certainly all be understood as being triple in meter $(2 + 2 + 2)$, since patterns such as ⌊♩ ♪♪♩⌋ are simply not part of the Viennese classical style. But in the case of fifteenth-century music the tradition of performance is lost. We are not sure how this music was performed and how these temporal relationships are to be articulated. Consequently, style cannot be taken for granted. Indeed, the problem of style is precisely the one which must be solved.

Our choices between the possible alternatives depend first of all upon internal evidence. For instance, where a clear structural parallelism exists between equivocal organizations and unequivocal ones, the latter may serve to determine the organization of the former. And these choices will seem the more plausible if it can be shown that they yield a convincing and self-consistent picture of the procedures of the work as a whole, making sense not only of the relationships within sections but also of those between sections. Such choices must, however, also be supported by external evidence. The analysis must, that is, not only be self-consistent; it must also be consistent with what we know about the style from other studies of works of this period and style. Finally, if the analysis is correct, it should be possible—although beyond the scope of this book—to relate the general aesthetic tendencies it exhibits to the aesthetic ideals and practices of other arts of the early Renaissance.

Let us begin by considering the first two measures. In the first measure the cantus part is unmistakably in triple meter. The second measure is apparently in duple meter; the sixteenth-note D is clearly an upbeat to the D which follows it, and the second D is accented on the lowest level.

The countertenor is in duple meter in measures 1 and 2. Thus it creates a metric dissonance ($\frac{(2+2)+2}{3+3}$) in the first measure which is resolved to a metric consonance ($\frac{3+3}{3+3}$) in the second measure. Since we know from the studies of Goldthwaite and others that such metric crossing is a common procedure in this style of music, the analysis given seems convincing.

The meter of the cantus in measure 3 is more doubtful. Two considerations make it seem probable that it should be interpreted in triple meter. In the first place, the melodic motion is such that the E sounds like an escape-note (échappée) moving to the A. Without this melodic inflection the grouping might have been duple, as it is in measure 13. Second, as we shall see, this interpretation fits with the alternation of duple and triple meter which runs through the entire piece. That is, the pattern of the cantus in the first eight measures runs like this: 3–2 3–2 3–3–2–2.

The meter of the countertenor is also open to question in measure 3. But if we consider its relationship to the tenor, a melodic parallelism seems clear. The parts are moving in thirds. Hence it seems plausible to regard the A as the accented note of the subgroup and to consider the C an escape-note. This analysis has the further advantage of being consistent with the one given for a similar type of melodic motion in the cantus. If such an interpretation is correct, then the meter of the countertenor would be duple— $(3 + 3)$. This is all the more convincing because measure 3 is now similar to measure 1, being a metric dissonance which is resolved to a consonance in measure 4.

Since only one voice moves in measure 4, the measure is metrically consonant. However, the triple meter of the countertenor is somewhat problematical. For this is the only measure in the whole countertenor part which is not in duple meter (3 + 3). The explanation of the change would seem to be that a simple duple meter would at this point have produced so great a letdown of tension that the two halves of the larger section (measure 1–8) would fall apart, becoming almost disconnected, separate entities. In short, the triple meter serves to maintain tension without creating metric dissonance.

In the second phrase the tenor has exactly the same temporal scheme as it had in the first phrase and the cantus begins as it did in measure 1. This clear parallelism suggests that the countertenor is *not* in triple meter ♩ ♫♩ (2 + 2 + 2) but in duple meter ♩ ♪♪♩ (3 + 3). The hypothesis that measure 5 involves metric crossing is supported by the fact that measure 6 is consonant. The parallelism between phrases (particularly in the tenor) also makes it probable that in measure 7 there is metric crossing which is resolved in measure 8, that is, that the cantus in measure 7 is not to be understood as a syncopated triple meter but as a duple meter ♪♪ ♩ ♩ (3 + 3), which crosses the triple meter of the tenor. On the other hand, the marked harmonic motion of the tenor, moving in six-three chords, tends to influence our perception of the cantus, so that it appears somewhat syncopated.

The meter of the countertenor is open to question, particularly since the metric crossing is already present in the other voices. However, because of the prevailing duple meter in this voice, it has been thus notated in Example 123. Moreover, from a melodic point of view a return to E on a beat, which would result if the meter were triple, does not seem convincing. That is, the melodic structure

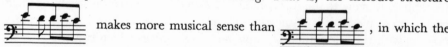 makes more musical sense than , in which the

D acts only as a changing-note rather than as a structural tone. On the other hand, an interpretation in triple meter which would parallel the motion of the tenor is a definite possibility.

Notice, however, that the parallelism between the first and second phrases is not exact. Although the tenor is the same in both parts and the procedure of metric crossing is similar, the metric structure of the cantus changes in measures 5–8. In the first half, metric alternation takes place every other measure: triple–duple–triple–duple. In the second phrase, metric alternation is by two-measure units: triple–triple–duple–duple(?). The question mark at the end of the scheme just given indicates that the organization of the second half of measure 8 is in doubt.

This leads us to a consideration of the metric organization of the passage beginning with the final tones of measure 8 and running through the beginning of measure 11. In these measures the meter of the cantus is particularly ambiguous and might be interpreted in various ways. Of the many groupings possible for this passage an examination of the pros and cons of four of the more plausible ones will, it is hoped, bring out some of the problems and considerations involved (Example 124).

EXAMPLE 124

The first alternative to be considered (Example 124*a*) has two things to recommend it: It continues the meter of the previous measures—although in a style in which metric change is normative, this is not necessarily a virtue; and it fits harmonically with the lower voices. Against this interpretation of the meter of the cantus are these considerations: The tone C does not become a point of metric-melodic culmination which it seems intended to be. And because the C is weak, the A's in measures 9, 10, and 11 are overemphasized. Furthermore, the syncopation of the C seems doubtful on both stylistic and purely musical grounds. In a style without marked pulses syncopation seems to have little function, and it is particularly pointless in this case, since there is no harmonic motion across the "bar line" to imbue the C with a need for motion. Finally, it should be observed that this alternative has little relationship to either the pattern of changing and crossing meters which precedes it or the clear triple meter which follows it.

The second alternative (Example 124*b*) does make metric sense when considered as part of a total metric scheme. In the first half of Section A the meter of the cantus changes after six eighth-notes—1(3 × 2) + 1(2 × 3); it changes after twelve eighth-notes in the second half of Section A—2(3 × 2) + 2(2 × 3); and, if the cantus were triple in the first half of Section B, then this progressive increase of distance between changes of meter would be continued, resulting in this scheme—3(3 × 2) + 3(2 × 3). Thus a very neat over-all metric progression of 1:2:3 is produced. Unfortunately, however, Example 124*b* is not convincing harmonically and melodically. From a harmonic point of view, the third and fourth groups of two (those beginning on G and B) are dissonant with the lower parts. Again the C fails to achieve what it would seem should be its melodic importance. And finally the syncopation is, as noted above, stylistically doubtful.

As indicated by the beam connecting the two C's across the bar, Example 124*c* is not syncopated. Furthermore, it does place a metric accent (on the lowest level) on the C, making it a point of melodic culmination. However, this version is objectionable on the ground that the first group of three (beginning on G) is dissonant. And beginning such a group on a dissonance seems doubtful on the basis of what we know of other works in this style. While this version of the passage does make some metric sense in relation to the rest of the piece and to the practice of the style, its symmetrical organization—

—does not really reflect the mode of progression previously established.

The final alternative (Example 124*d*) works both harmonically and melodically. The groups of twos and threes all begin on consonances and the high C comes at the beginning of such a metric group. Although this version is metrically more complex than Example 124*c*, it does reflect the metric *modus operandi* of the first section of the piece. Indeed it is in a sense a condensed presentation of that section. That is, its organization (2 + 3, 2 + 3, 2 + 2, 3 + 3) presents an accelerated version of the pattern of metric change between measures which took place in the opening section. Moreover, the condensation is not only metric but melodic as well. For the motion from D to C encompasses the basic range of the first section of the piece. And this emphasizes again the necessity for the C to arrive on an accent, as it did in measure 6 and as do both the A in measure 11 and the B-flat in measure 12, to which it moves.

Finally, the metric complexity of this version of the passage with its intensification of metric change seems appropriate in view of the fact that the passage is clearly intended to be one of tension and motion. For it is so constructed that no matter which of the alternatives examined above is chosen, two measures of metric dissonance result. Thus measures 9 and 10 function as metric dissonances resolving to the metric consonance of the final three measures which are solidly in duple meter.

It is clear that both metric change and metric crossing are basic principles of organization here. They are so not only in their own right but also in the sense that they articulate and influence the rhythmic structure of the whole piece.

EXAMPLE 125

For instance, metric crossing in measures 1, 3, 5, and 7 makes those measures anacrustic to measures 2, 4, 6, and 8, respectively. Similarly, the metric structure of the first part of Section B forms the basis for the anapestic rhythm which arises in these measures, while the metric crossing between parts articulates the rhythm of the second architectonic level. These matters as well as the rhythmic organization on all levels should be clear from the analysis given in Example 125.

EXERCISES

I

A. Analyze the following passages on all architectonic levels:

    Bach, Chamber Suite No. 4 in D Major, iii, 1–10

    ———, Prelude and Fugue in A Major for Organ, Fugue, 1–16

Bartók, Piano Sonata (1926), i, 1–13
————, Violin Concerto, i, 6–15
Beethoven, Bagatelle Op. 119 No. 1, 53–64
————, Piano Sonata Op. 111, i, 19–29
Binchois, "De plus en plus" (*Historical Anthology of Music*, ed. Archibald T. Davison and Willi Apel [Cambridge, Mass.: Harvard University Press, 1947], I, 74)
Brahms, Sonata in D Minor for Violin and Piano, i, 48–56
————, String Quartet in A Minor, i, 162–64
Chopin, Etude Op. 10 No. 10, 1–16
————, Etude Op. 25 No. 8, 1–4
Handel, Concerto Grosso No. 7 in B-flat Major, v, 1–7
Haydn, "London" Symphony in D Major, iii, 21–26
————, String Quartet Op. 77 No. 2, ii, 1–24
Mozart, Sonata in A Major for Violin and Piano (K. 305), i, 24–28
Schubert, Impromptu Op. 142 No. 4, 45–77
Schumann, String Quartet Op. 44 No. 1, ii, 1–6
————, Symphony No. 1 in B-flat Major, iii, 1–16
Stravinsky, Suite No. 2 for Small Orchestra, ii, 23–30

B. Write a brief essay about each passage discussing the relationship of rhythm to meter. How does your understanding of this relationship influence your interpretation of the music in performance? Where alternative interpretations seem possible, discuss how each alternative would affect performance.

II

A. Find themes illustrating the following: (1) stressed weak beats, (2) melodic-metric non-congruence, (3) syncopation, suspension, and tie, (4) potential accents made to function as weak beats, and (5) metric-rhythmic crossing.

B. Analyze each of these themes and write a brief essay discussing each theme and your analysis of it. How does the metric-rhythmic organization affect the character of the theme?

III. Write a theme and variations in which each of the following is exemplified in one of the variations: (1) stressed weak beats, (2) metric-melodic non-congruence, (3) syncopation, (4) potential accents forced to act as weak beats, and (5) metric-rhythmic crossing.

V RHYTHM, MOBILITY, AND TENSION

Paradoxically, every analysis of a piece of music is a kind of synthesis. We have seen again and again in these pages how important to our analysis of rhythm can be our understanding of the melody, the harmony, the tone-color, and the dynamics of the music in question. In this chapter and the next, texture and form will be added to those aspects of music which must be taken into account if rhythm is to be properly understood. Texture and form, however, are not the only—or even the main—topics of these chapters.

If this were a book about melody, we should find that our analysis of melody would imply an understanding of many things other than melody; it is plain that harmony cannot be treated successfully apart from texture (at the very least); and so on, for any kind of analysis directed at one specific aspect of music. At its best, the analysis of one musical factor describes the effects of all the factors in combination. It describes these effects, but it by no means does each of them full justice. There are two main reasons for this. First, any system of analysis uses symbols, and symbols simplify by classifying. This is true even if words alone are used. One must guard against mistaking classification for the end of analysis. The end of analysis is the appreciation of the peculiar, the individual. In fact, the peculiar individuality of a good piece of music is the second main reason why analysis, however thoughtful, does incomplete justice to music. Aside from the fact that a whole is more than a sum of its parts, the various aspects of music do not necessarily coincide in their effects on any one architectonic level.[1] Indeed, a conflict of effect can be an important source of the peculiar individuality of which we have been speaking.

RHYTHM AND MOBILITY

Let us examine the familiar opening of the finale in Mozart's "Jupiter" symphony (Example 126).

Partly because of tonality, some of the notes in the melody are more mobile

[1] See the discussion of Example 11, p. 17; see also the remarks on performance, p. 18.

than others. Mobility means the sense that further melodic motion is necessary
in order to reach a point of relative repose, a goal of melodic movement. In
the Mozart fragment (Example 126*a*), the notes D and F are more mobile than
the notes with which they are associated, C and E. There are two reasons for
this. First, C and E are notes in the tonic triad. In a passage in C major, therefore, they tend to be pitches from which and to which melody moves as from one
relatively stable point to another. Of course, this relative stability is not a matter
of melody alone. The harmony may alter the tonal significance of the melody and
make otherwise relatively stable notes more mobile (see the last measure of
Example 126*d*). The second reason why D and F are more mobile here than C

EXAMPLE 126

and E is that the D, following the C, sets up a direction of melodic movement;
it gives us the feeling that the melody is on its way to a point not yet reached:
certainly to E, and perhaps beyond it. The note F sidesteps the direct line of
motion from C to E. Moving from D to F creates a gap in that line of motion,
and this gap increases the desirability of E as a goal of motion; it makes the F
lean heavily on the E and require resolution there. The F is mobile because of its
function in the melodic line.

The mobile F is accented. The goal of motion, E, is not accented. One is
tempted to say that the E has a *melodic* accent, even though it is rhythmically an
afterbeat. But each aspect of the music qualifies all the others, and it would be
more in accord with one's experience of this passage to say that the E *with an
F leaning on it* is melodically marked for consciousness. It is the accented-F-
leaning-on-E that is in large part responsible for the peculiarity of these four
measures. Notice, however, that it is what happens in the first two measures

which makes possible the effect of what happens in the last two. To generalize, unaccent is an aspect of accent, and a rhythmic group is an accented shape.

Compare *c* with *a* in Example 126. In *c*, melodic goal, harmonic goal, and rhythmic accent all coincide (measure 3). In *a*, melody and harmony are mobile at the accent (measure 3) and relatively static at the afterbeat (measure 4). For harmony, like melody, has its moments of relative mobility and stability. In Example 126*c*, the dominant chord of measure 2 sets up, or seeks to move toward, a tonic chord. Measures 3 and 4 follow as the normal thing from 1 and 2. Measures 3 and 4 of Example 126*c* would not, however, follow as the normal thing from measures 1 and 2 of Example 126*a*. There, the II$^6_5$ chord of measure 2 sets up some kind of dominant as the next chord. That is, one expects a relatively mobile harmony in measure 3, rather than the far more static tonic which occurs at the corresponding place in Example 126*c*. What happens harmonically in measures 1 and 2 of Example 126*a* makes what happens harmonically and melodically in measures 3 and 4 appropriate. (Let us not make the mistake of saying "inevitable.") The F in measure 3 is appropriate harmonically, because it is part of a V^7 chord which follows as a goal of movement from the previous II$^6_5$ chord. This V^7 chord, in its turn, is highly mobile, and marks the following chord (VI instead of I) for consciousness. But just as we characterized the goal of melodic movement here as accented-F-leaning-on-E, so we may characterize the goal of harmonic movement as accented-V^7-leaning-on-VI. And it is VI on which V^7 leans here. If the reader finds this difficult to believe, let him try to put a tonic triad in root position in measure 4 in such a way that the second violins are forced to do nothing awkward either in voice-leading or in playing technique.

If we add another part as in Example 126*b*, two things happen. First, we become decidedly conscious of the normal harmonic tendency for the V^7 chord to resolve onto a tonic triad, and of the melodic and harmonic tendency in this passage for the F to move to an E, because these tendencies are forced upon us by the dissonances between treble and bass. The music becomes tied down and loses the floating, bass-less quality of the original. Second, the texture becomes stylistically more normal. These two things happen without any outward result in an analysis on the first level—and perhaps even on the second—but they have an important bearing on a feeling for the rhythm. Let us examine this feeling before taking further steps.

The art of analysis is based upon the art of listening. In analyzing Example 126, we are reflecting, with symbols, upon our experience in listening to the beginning of a classical finale (and various distortions thereof). In listening to such a piece we do not leave our knowledge of classical finales out of account. Even if we pretend that we know nothing about this particular movement, we nevertheless know quite a lot about it. For example, it is going to contain passages that are loud, in at least four-part harmony, and for full orchestra. What we are listening to now (*a*) is soft, in three-part harmony, and for violins alone. If some sophist interrupts us at this point to refer to the finale of Haydn's "Farewell" Symphony, we know what to tell him. The important thing here is that we know perfectly well that what we are now hearing is leading up to something of a certain kind. No matter how sure we may be at the moment (say, at the end of measure 4) that this whole phrase is accented, it nevertheless has about it a strong background feeling of anticipation—in other words, an upbeat feeling. Now this is not the same thing as calling it an upbeat phrase. Perhaps a larger section of which these four measures are only the beginning will function on a higher architectonic level as an anacrusis. Perhaps just this phrase will so function. We do not yet know. We know only that this phrase is ready, as a whole, to be in retrospect an anacrusis, or an accented part of a larger anacrusis, or an unaccented part of a larger anacrusis.

In version *b* the texture is less abnormal; the harmony is less mobile; indeed, the phrase is in itself more stable than the original, although it is still ready to be in retrospect an anacrusis or a part of one. The feeling about it of anticipation is less, however. And this feeling can be made lesser: for instance, by making a crescendo in measures 1 and 2 to a forte in measure 3, and by orchestrating measure 3 as a tutti with various octave doublings. The analysis on the first level remains the same, but the rhythm feels different. Version *b* might be followed by the same thing that follows version *a* in the actual symphony. If so, the analysis on the second level as well would remain the same, but the rhythm, again, would feel different.

In version *c* both melody and harmony move along straight paths. Imagine the passage forte and with a tutti accompaniment from measure 2 onward. It can still become in retrospect an anacrusis or a part of one, but in itself—that is, until something else follows—it is the most positively accented of the four versions.

Version *d*, on the other hand, is the least positively accented of the four. Both *a* and *d* end with a deceptive cadence, but the final chord in *d* is more specifically mobile than is the final chord in *a*. The demand that something follow *d* is more specific and clear; the demand that something follow *a* is more general and vague, however strong it may be.

In making an analysis on the primary rhythmic level, then, we are by implication making a potential analysis on the higher levels, and, in a real sense, we are beginning to assess the individuality of the whole.

Let us now turn to a more complex structure in the same work, the beginning of the first movement, in order to make a similar analysis and carry it to higher architectonic levels (Example 127).

In the reiterated and powerful C's of the first two measures we have a feeling quite different from the one generated by the melodic motion from C to D in the first two measures of Example 126*a*. There, direction of movement was immediately established. Here, there is no such thing. The music is solidly planted on the tonic in an end-accented rhythm. It is going to move on a larger scale; it is going to have a slower pace. We anticipate movement, but we do not yet know its direction. And then, before anything happens to this opening motive, we are presented with a violent contrast in measures 3 and 4. This is a contrast in dynamics, in texture, in orchestration, and altogether in character.

Now measures 1 and 2 and measures 3 and 4 are both connected and disconnected. They are connected in part simply because they are next to each other. A composer's imagination must often present him with such seemingly accidental

EXAMPLE 127

juxtapositions of ideas. What becomes of this particular juxtaposition we shall see shortly. The forte idea and the piano idea are further connected by the very fact that the piano idea moves both melodically and harmonically, and we had anticipated movement. Besides that, as the analysis on level 1 shows, the rhythms of the two ideas are similar: each is end-accented, and each has three "syllables." But we are more struck by the disconnection, the contrast. In place of the tonic we have the dominant (the tonic triad in the middle of measure 3 being a passing-chord, very unemphatic rhythmically); in place of the uncompromising C's we have the movement from C to G-leaning-on-F.

The quasi-turn around C followed by a leap to F preceded by an appoggiatura should be compared for its effect of relative mobility with the melody of Example 126*a*. There, C was relatively stable and F was highly mobile. Here, C is highly mobile, although it is the tonic, and F, because it is the goal of motion, is relatively stable (within these two measures, that is), in spite of its general tonal mobility and, more important, in spite of its being the seventh in a dominant-seventh chord. Broadly speaking, the relative mobility of the notes C and F is more peculiar here than it is in the finale.

How does this reversal of the normal tonal roles of C and F in C major come about? The first C (that at the end of measure 2) is underplayed rhythmically: it is an anticipation. The second C is underplayed harmonically: it is a dissonant appoggiatura. The third C is again underplayed rhythmically: although it is a resolution, and consonant, it occurs on an unaccent on the subprimary level. So much for the C. What of the F? The melody leaps boldly (because unexpectedly) to G, and this G is perfectly consonant with the rest of the harmony. Yet not only is it treated as an appoggiatura; one feels it has to be so treated. The reason for this feeling lies in the rhythm on the subprimary level. There we have, first, two *attempted* amphibrachs. The dissonances on the first and third beats of measure 3 would normally be resolved on afterbeats, but the resolutions are delayed in such a way as to turn them into upbeats. Our desire to hear an afterbeat is frustrated in measure 3, and when the melody moves to G, this desire is only the stronger for having been twice frustrated. The rhythm, that is, forces the G to resolve on the F. And this rhythmic effect is so powerful that it makes us hear a consonant note (G) as a dissonance and a dissonant note (F) as a consonance—so powerful, indeed, as to make the nominal V$_3^6$ chord in the middle of measure 4 stand in no need of resolution onto a tonic triad with the third on top.

It would be instructive at this point to look ahead to Example 128*a*, in which the amphibrachs on the subprimary level are "allowed." You will notice that, try as you may, you cannot follow the final G of this example with an F without having it sound like a ludicrous error.

It is not, however, only the rhythm on the subprimary level which creates the peculiarity of the F as a melodic goal of movement. It is also the bold leap to G, presumably part of what was given by the composer's imagination. Let us suppose the composer to have been a far lesser one and glance ahead at Example 129*a*. There we can see the same rhythmic effect, as far as the analysis would show, as in the original, but the rhythm has done nothing at all drastic to our feeling for melodic mobility. Given the melodic direction set up in the first measure of Example 129*a*, there is nothing in the least peculiar about having a D as the goal of movement in the next measure.

If we now go on and listen to the whole of the first eight measures of the movement, we notice at once that we are uncertain of how to group them on the second level. On the one hand, measures 1–4 and 5–8 stand in an antecedent-consequent relationship; they use the same motives in the same order, and the harmonic movement from tonic to dominant in the antecedent is answered by a movement from dominant to tonic in the consequent. We can therefore group measures 1–4 together, and measures 5–8. On the other hand, the contrast between the two motives is sufficiently strong so that one cannot help also grouping the two forte passages together and the two piano passages. The grouping on the second level is ambiguous. It is for this reason that we have put a question mark there in the analysis. Although the two forte passages together and the two piano passages together will both be end-accented groups, the two groups will have different feelings on the next level. The forte group will feel like an upbeat, since it moves harmonically from tonic to dominant, and the piano group will be ambiguous, since, although it moves harmonically from dominant to tonic and is to that extent accented, it is only partially complete melodically: the movement from C to F in measures 3–4 and continuing, again from C, through F to G in measures 7–8, only succeeds in pointing to the higher C as the next desired note and thus tinges the harmonically accented aspect of the group with a feeling of anacrusis.

The skeletal analysis on the bottom staff of Example 127 is intended to show that both the piano groups and the forte groups point melodically at C's for their sense of completion. With the entrance of the tutti in measure 9, the ambiguity we have been previously feeling about the grouping is brilliantly removed, and we are able in retrospect to make a satisfying grouping on the third level. The analysis on that level under Example 127 indicates both the somewhat unstable antecedent-consequent relationship mentioned earlier and the retrospective grouping with measure 9 as its accent.

In the discussion of Example 126, mention was made of the important part played in our feeling for rhythm on higher levels by our general knowledge of the particular style in which a piece of music is written. It is worth while to revert to this notion in considering Example 127. Is it not true that while we are listening to measures 1–8 we are aware in the back of our minds that there is going to be (we do not know exactly when) a tutti in the full texture of the Viennese style? When we hear that tutti enter in measure 9, it is not an unexpected event. But notice that it has a rhythmic function, that of clarifying the grouping of measures 1–8; it is motivated. It is not only normal; it is also right. Of such congruences is music made.

It should be clear from this example that dynamics, texture, orchestration, and character, as well as melody and harmony, can play important parts in the analysis of rhythm. Indeed, a satisfactory rhythmic analysis can be said in some sense to summarize the effects of these factors. This is not to say that rhythmic analysis is the only tool of generalization in thinking about music—as we shall see in the next chapter—but it is an important one, and we can gain some further insight into its generalizing powers by worrying the bone of Example 127 a bit more before going on.

What would be the consequences of replacing measures 3–4 of Example 127 with Example 128*a?* The only satisfactory answer we could get to the melodic question C–G would be the G–C of Example 128*b,* which would then appear in measures 7–8 of the original. This would be embarrassingly feeble. The piano parts would be both harmonically and melodically finished, while the forte parts remained up in the air. The continuation in measure 9 would be satisfying as far as the forte parts are concerned but redundant otherwise. (Never mind the fussy, waspish character of Example 128.)

Or let us try replacing the piano parts of the original with the entirely normal and perfectly logical *a* and *b* of Example 129. The same difficulty would be upon us as in Example 128. Perhaps we could create a feeling of anacrusis by inserting a B-flat as in Example 129*c*. So far, so good, but then we could not go on as in measure 9 of the original, since the next thing indicated would seem to be a six-four chord over C in the bass. All that these remarks signify is that what Mozart

EXAMPLE 128

EXAMPLE 129

EXAMPLE 130

did in Example 127 is right and that we have been unable to tinker with it without making it wrong. This does not mean at all that Mozart might not have done something else that would have been right. It means only that measures 1–8 as Mozart wrote them have a certain rhythmic quality (compounded of all the various aspects of the music) and that this quality makes the continuation of the music in measure 9 convincing.

Perhaps we should have tried doing something to the forte parts, as in Example 130. This time, the forte parts will be finished and the piano parts will remain in the air, making the tutti of measure 9 again partly and unpleasantly redundant. Or we could go all the way and combine Example 129*a* and *b* with Example 130. Now nothing will follow. Measure 9 will simply be more music; it will no longer be the right music; there would be no right music.

The reader should notice carefully that all these unpleasant alterations which we have made would result in exactly the same analysis on the primary level as in Example 127. It is not so much what occurs *rhythmically* on the primary level that determines what we feel on the higher levels, as it is what occurs in the other aspects of music. This is why rhythmic analysis has such a strong generalizing power.

Before leaving the first movement of the "Jupiter" Symphony, let us look at a genuine alteration of the material we have been considering—genuine, because made by the composer himself in the course of composition. In Example 131

EXAMPLE 131

changes have been made which result in complete clarity of grouping on the second level. The dynamics, the texture, and the orchestration have been made more homogeneous, with the result that the original contrast in character has been softened. Furthermore, the contrapuntal accompaniment, with its complete continuity of rhythm (see analysis 1*a*), has bound together the whole four measures into something that can be heard as a single group without forcing the original rhythms on the primary level to lose their individual identity. Of course this new rhythm for old material will allow a different continuation, as an examination of the score will show.

RHYTHM AND TENSION

We have been discussing movement in music and the issue of this movement in the generalized feeling we call rhythm. The time has come to examine the feeling more analytically.

The possible elements in a rhythmic group are upbeat (or anacrusis), accent, and afterbeat. No one of these feels like the others, nor does any one of them itself always feel the same. But before attempting to generalize further, let us proceed inductively by examining selections from four pieces.

The first is Chopin's Prelude in E-flat (Example 132). Throughout most of this Prelude the fundamental rhythm is a middle-accented one. But this rhythm seldom appears as a grouping of three quarter-notes; usually, the anacrusis is lengthened. At the beginning of the piece, for instance (Example 132*a* and *a'*), the anacrusis sails up from the B-flat to the G with a sense of continuous movement through an unobstructed arpeggio and without any minor groupings except for that of the opening B-flat and its anticipation. One might call this anacrusis a lyrical one, or, perhaps, a contemplative one. The feeling which arises from it is rather like that which arises from seeing a speeded-up moving picture of a bud gradually opening into a flower. The tension[2] with which we await the appearance of the full-blown flower is rather like the tension with which we await the reversal of movement (to F and E-flat) in measure 3 of the Prelude; it is a tension of calm rather than one of agitation. Other than rubato, there is no temporal differentiation here. Nothing happens harmonically until measure 3. There is no dynamic change except the slight crescendo which seems to be natural in a rising melodic line.

EXAMPLE 132

Obviously, the performer must see to it that the E-flat (second beat of measure 1) is not closer in time to the preceding B-flat than it is to the following G; if necessary, the B-flat on the first beat of measure 1 can be held slightly beyond its time in order that the following E-flat will not sound like the end of a group. And, in general, the performer cannot afford to play according to the unthinking principle, "stress the first beat of the bar," or he will readily fall into a constant subsidiary amphibrach grouping. Chopin, for him, might as well have written as in Example 132*b* and *b'*. The contemplative tension of the initial anacrusis is an essential part of the character of this piece.

As we can see in Example 133, Chopin can achieve a lengthened anacrusis by means other than unchanging harmony and uninhibited upward melodic movement. In measure 5, there is the auxiliary note D in the melody; two measures later, this D is associated with a B in the accompaniment. These dissonances compel us to make two-measure groupings. Of course, the performer merely has to think in the groupings indicated by the analysis; he will then, provided he has adequate technical habits, automatically achieve correct results.

[2] We wish we could use the word "intensity," but it has been pre-empted for the description of dynamics.

In the Chopin excerpts we have just been considering, the elements of melody and harmony conspire in a single, simple rhythmic effect, and the dynamics are those most natural to this effect: the slight crescendo on an anacrusis and the gentle decrescendo on an accent followed by an afterbeat. In the following excerpt from the same composer's Etude Op. 10 No. 9 (Example 134), the case is quite different. Instead of serene lyricism we find a dramatic conflict which has much to do with the rather petulant character of the music.

This conflict appears first on the primary and secondary rhythmic levels. The

EXAMPLE 133

EXAMPLE 134

harmony consists in each measure of a set of appoggiaturas which resolve onto a tonic triad, over a tonic pedal which persists—and has persisted for some time—in the bass. The rhythm of the harmony, therefore, is trochaic. This becomes particularly clear if we examine the simplified version in Example 135*a*. But the melody of the original (see Example 134) is middle-accented in measures 57–58 and 61–62 and end-accented in the other measures. And each of the accents in the melody falls on the afterbeat of the accompaniment. Indeed, in measure 59 the conflict is aggravated by the crescendo placed on the anacrusis, which only succeeds in stressing the conflict in accent.

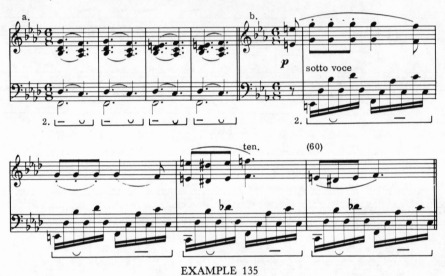

EXAMPLE 135

The reader will notice that if we rewrite the passage according to the pattern of Example 135*b* the conflict disappears, for both melody and harmony are now end-accented. At the same time, the character has changed radically. The outbursts in measures 61 and 63, for instance, have become assertive and positive, and have lost their air of trying to escape from enforced suppression. The rhythmic conflict of the original is essential to the character of the music.

On the third architectonic level there are lyrical afterbeats; the even-numbered measures echo the odd-numbered ones. These echoing afterbeats have the effect of lowering the "temperature" of the music—of releasing the tension of the music while they echo. And the dynamics on this level are not in conflict with the rhythm. The echoes are softer than what is echoed. On the next level, however, there is again dramatic conflict; for again we have echoes, but this time the dynamics are against the echo effect. Measures 59–60 echo measures 57–58 with variations; likewise, measures 63–64 echo measures 61–62. But in measure 59 there is a return to the piano of measure 57, after an intervening pianissimo, and this piano is followed by a crescendo; the dynamics of the echo are stronger than those of the echoed. And the situation is more striking in measure 63, with its fortissimo following upon the forte-pianissimo of the previous measures.

Finally, on the highest architectonic level indicated in the analysis, the second four measures echo the first four; yet it is in the echo that we find forte and fortissimo. Furthermore, it is here that the upbeats on the primary level are more loaded with tension; there are simply more notes in the upbeats. In the case of the G's, the increased reiteration and the downward leap of an octave indicate a greater frenzy, one might say, in reaching the accent, and this accent can never be a positive one, coming as it does against the feminine rhythm of the harmony. In like manner, the upbeats in measures 63–64 may move farther on their way from E to F, but it is still from E to F that they move.

One can learn a good deal about the peculiarity of this passage by some interchanging of parts. For instance, the reader might play the same notes but interchange the dynamics of measures 57–60 and 61–64. He will find that because the effect of the lyrical afterbeat of measures 61–64 is not contradicted by the dynamics the character is significantly different. Or, again, he might interchange measures 57–60 and 61–64 completely. In this case, the result will sound offensively wrong, because measures 57–60, thus misplaced, become an insipid oversimplification of measures 61–64, instead of a relaxed echo of them.

Not every afterbeat on a higher architectonic level is of the sort we have been describing as "lyrical." A lyrical afterbeat is one which echoes a point of arrival, a goal of motion. In the example under discussion, the goal of motion is reached in measure 57. Compared with what happens in that measure, there is, we may say, no further motion at all.[3]

AN EXTENDED ANACRUSIS

In the excerpts we have examined so far in this chapter, the effects of rhythmic grouping have extended over relatively short spaces of time. We now turn to a much longer excerpt, which, in spite of its length, is readily heard as an anapest which embodies an exciting climax. The excerpt (Example 136) is from the introduction to Act II of Wagner's *Tristan und Isolde*.

The large group to be considered begins in measure 33, but a few of the previous measures have been included in the example in order to make clear one of the peculiarities of the rhythm. This peculiarity is that there is a conflict in the sense of movement which arises from the passage beginning in measure 33. Both the characteristic quarter-note motion of the cello melody in the previous

---

[3] Example 92 in chapter iii contains an excellent case of a lyrical afterbeat. Note the effect of all four afterbeats on the second level.

EXAMPLE 136

EXAMPLE 136—*Continued*

EXAMPLE 136—*Continued*

measures and the agitated accompaniment figure in the upper strings suddenly disappear, leaving a rapid, largely eighth-note motion in the melody and a much slower motion in the accompaniment. This conflict between a slow substratum and an agitated surface is appropriate to the dramatic situation which will be disclosed when the curtain rises, inasmuch as it sets the agitation in high relief. The analyses on level 1 and level 2*b* are to be read simultaneously as an indication of the two rhythms. The analysis of the rhythm on the subprimary level (which is easy to make) has been omitted in the interest of clarity.

Now the underlying rhythm (level 2*b*) of measures 33–38 is primarily dependent upon harmonic movement. We have first a diminished-seventh chord acting as dominant of II, followed by II^6 with an appoggiatura, F-sharp, which resolves to G. This makes the amphibrach of measures 33–34. After this, the II^6 chord is altered (E-flat to E and C to C-sharp) so as to lead toward a I$^6_4$ chord which would, of course, tend to resolve onto a dominant of some form or other. This sequence of chords, along with the resulting underlying rhythm, is indicated in the variant in Example 136. We see that the rhythm of measures 33–38 would be two amphibrachs pivoted together into one group; the second amphibrach would take twice as much time as the first. In the actual music, however, the I$^6_4$ chord does not appear; the harmony moves directly, in measure 37, to a dominant-ninth (flatted). The reader might object that of course the chord in measures 36–37 moves to a dominant, inasmuch as the C-sharp is really a D-flat. But that would be to overlook the melody in the oboe, which would have to read in measure 35: E-double-flat–D-flat–G–E–B-flat–G–E–E-double-flat (!). More important, it would be to overlook the tremendously liberating effect of the I$^6_4$ chord in measure 71, which is preceded by four measures of this very chord (E–G–B-flat–C-sharp) with the C-sharp, to be sure, written as a D-flat. This I$^6_4$ chord, with a subsequent dominant, is the harmonic goal of the whole passage.

Because of the omission of the I$^6_4$ chord, the rhythm in measures 35–38 remains incomplete (level 2*b*): there are simply two unaccents. But the whole six measures are a single pivoted group, in spite of the incomplete rhythm. This is partly because of the rhythm on the subprimary level; but more of a part is played here by the overlapping instrumentation–flute, oboe, clarinet.

It is the very incompleteness of the rhythm which is primarily responsible for turning measures 33–38 into an anacrusis (level 2*b*)—rather, into part of an anacrusis. To be sure, the monstrosity in the variant would be an anacrusis also, because of its dominant ending. But notice that the variant is an antecedent phrase. Upon hearing it, one would not anticipate a long wait before hearing the consequent phrase designed to answer it. In the actual music, measures 33–38 are not an antecedent phrase. Try to imagine a consequent starting at measure 39, and you will see that the rhythmic difficulty—that of "answering" an incomplete rhythm—puts it out of the question. No, what we have here is a pure anacrusis, not a phrase from a formal theme. The theme, if one wishes to stretch the meaning of the term, extends over the entire excerpt.

The passage we have been listening to turns out to be an anacrusis to an anacrusis. Measures 39–42 are the two upbeats of an anapest, the second upbeat being continued in a syncopation which stretches through measures 43–44, so as to lead to the heavy second-level accent beginning in measure 45. But this accent, after being clearly shaped almost to the end of measure 46, loses itself in, again, an incomplete rhythm of enormous tension which leads, in turn, to what we expect to be an accent on the beginning of measure 50. Thus, measures 39–49 have gone the way of measures 33–38; that is, they have begun with a clear rhythmic shape, but they have ended with an incomplete rhythm, and what was going to be a rhythm turns into a part of a rhythm, namely, an anacrusis.

Before leaving this anacrusis, a comparison should be made between measures 39–42 and Example 134. Both passages contain echoes, but Wagner's echoes are parts of upbeats; Chopin's are afterbeats. This difference comes about, however, not simply through position, that is, through coming at the beginning of a group rather than at the end of one. Harmony is in fact vital in creating the difference. Put in the simplest terms, Chopin's harmony is all tonic; Wagner's is all ambiguous. Wagner has two diminished-seventh chords in parallel motion a wholestep apart; they have no clear tonal function; a sense of tonality first appears with the augmented-sixth chord at the beginning of measure 43. In Chopin, all has been reached; in Wagner, all is yet to be reached.

We think we are going to reach something when we get to measure 50 of Example 136. But, although the chord is the right chord, the dynamics are unexpected.

First, about the chord; it is, of course, the same as the one introduced in measure 35. We can see how right it is if we omit measures 50–66 and go directly from measure 49 to measure 67, after which we shall shortly hear the resolution of this chord to the I_4^6 which the harmony of measures 35–36 failed to reach. The chord, then, announces what the goal of the large anacrusis will in part be like. It also announces, however, that it is not that goal. It does this by its dynamics. (Notice also the subtle absence of tremolo in measure 50.)

Now, about the dynamics: if we look back to measures 29–32, we find, in the top line, an introduction to the passage beginning in measure 33. The introduction is piano crescendo. The crescendo leads to a sudden pianissimo at the beginning of measure 33. This sudden pianissimo is in part responsible for our feeling that something begins here. Now, when we arrive at measure 50 and find that it is unexpectedly piano, we remember the previous feeling of beginning attached to measure 33, and we have the feeling of beginning again. This feeling is fully borne out by the fact that measures 50–66 are an almost note-for-note transposition of measures 33–49. For the piano of measure 50 is both unexpected (in view of the restless fortissimo anacrusis which precedes it) and prepared (by the piano–crescendo–pianissimo of measures 29–33). Furthermore, we can see from this passage that tremendous tension is not necessarily associated with loud dynamics. The piano of measure 50, with all its attendant air of "having to go through it all again," has the tension of delay, the tension of long lengths of time being welded into a single group, and, by the time we have reached the end of measure 66, we are aware that we have heard the two large anacruses of an over-riding anapest on the third level.

No sooner have we reached measure 67, however, than we realize that the large accent itself begins with an anacrusis (level 2). The fortissimo is there, and the chord of measures 34 and 50 is there, but the resolution is yet to come. The anacrusis is built up by echoes (level 1) in measures 67–70 without any harmonic movement. If we compare this passage with that in measures 39–42, we may say that they have a certain rhythmic similarity, in that both are upbeats in an anapest. But there the similarity ends. In the earlier passage, the music is moving somewhere, we know not where until we arrive. In the later passage, we know where we are going: we are going to a I_4^6 chord—finally. The quality of the tension is different here. It is the tension which arises from repetitions of a harmony that is mobile and has a specific direction. Yet this tremendous tension is capped, even at the very moment of its release, by the powerful appoggiatura G on the first beat of measure 71. And then, just as the G resolves, through G-flat, to F, we are back where we started from in measure 33.

How is the goal of movement, the I_4^6 chord, to reach the dominant on which it leans? It cannot do so immediately, because one cannot find release from excite-ment by pricking its balloon. Time is needed. And time is provided by means of a series of echoes, decrescendo. These echoes consist of truncated amphibrachs on the primary level. That much of the rhythm which is within measure 72— the accent and the afterbeat—is repeated three times in measures 73–75 in such a way that the sequence of harmonies—IV (measure 72), V (73), and twice I (74–75)—is created over a dominant pedal very low in the horns, each harmony being preceded by appoggiaturas. Thus the accent itself trails off, to begin with, in an incomplete rhythm on the second level. The incompleteness of the rhythm is emphasized by underplaying the continuity on the subprimary level. For, al-though there is overlapping among the winds, which double the strings here, the change of string color is striking, the string parts do not overlap, and the breaks between measures are clarified; therefore one does not hear a series of pivoted amphibrachs, with the afterbeat of one becoming the upbeat of the next, nor yet a series of trochees, but rather a series of echoes of ends of amphibrachs. The violins, which play the melody starting in measure 71, are cut off at the end of measure 72; there follow the violas, entirely within measure 72; violins again in

74; finally, the cellos in 75 are allowed to run over to the first beat of 76, where the awaited dominant appears, piano. Notice that measure 75 echoes measure 74 exactly in melody and harmony (though not in color and range), and that therefore a small anapest is created on the second level with the dominant chord at the beginning of measure 76 as its accent. In this manner, the second-level accent of measures 67–76 begins, as did the large third-level anacrusis, with a complete rhythm which is succeeded by an incomplete rhythm; only, this time the incomplete rhythm is itself succeeded by another complete rhythm at the end, so that the rhythmic impulse may conclude with a final accent.

Two things remain to be noticed about this excerpt.

First, the amount of energetic tension which has been built up in a wavelike fashion in the two upbeats (measures 33–49 and 50–66) on the third level is too great to be released in the relatively short accent (measures 67–76) which follows. Yet more time is needed. If the reader will refer to the score, he will find that the dominant pedal is sustained for a long time after our excerpt ends, while over it the six extra horns play their hunting calls behind the scenes. There then comes another wave—a receding one, as it were—made up of the same motives as are to be found in the excerpt, whereupon the music reverts to the hunting calls over the dominant pedal. The subsidence lasts quite long, and its generally static quality makes for a successful and much-needed anticlimax.

The other thing which must be noticed has to do with the relationship between the goal chord (I_4^6) of measure 71 and its chord of resolution (V) in measure 76. This relationship is unlike any to be found in all the previous examples in this book, with the exception of Example 86 in chapter iii. If the reader will turn back to that example (p. 69) he will recall that the accent on the third level consists of an amphibrach which arises from pivoting. The accent of this amphibrach falls on a I_4^6 chord, and the succeeding afterbeat consists (on the primary level) of an iamb on the progression V^7–I. Obviously, the afterbeat consists harmonically of the resolution of the accent. But the chord of final resolution (I) is separated from the accented chord (I_4^6); it does not follow immediately. Now imagine this relationship stretched in time so that several measures intervene between accented, mobile harmony and resolution and return to Example 136.

Here, we repeat, the I_4^6 chord in measure 71 is the (initially) accented goal of motion, a goal, however, which leans on a dominant, and this dominant, which is harmonically stable as compared to the I_4^6 chord, is widely separated from it in time. It has to be so separated because of the great stretches of time which go into the anapest on the third architectonic level. But beyond that, the way in which it is separated is appropriate to the pyramided grouping of the whole excerpt. In this pyramided grouping, incomplete rhythm has a prominent role. In the two third-level anacruses (measures 33–49 and 50–66) we have seen the importance of incomplete rhythm in creating a feeling of motion toward a goal and in stretching the lengths. The third-level accent is, itself, an anapest in which the anacruses consist, on the second level, of incomplete rhythms. And now we see also that the second-level accent of measures 71–76 itself contains incomplete rhythms which, however, are finally allowed to give way (in measures 74–76) to another anapestic grouping. In other words, the rhythmic procedure is homogeneous throughout: although the fundamental rhythm is the amphibrach, the fundamental shape is the anapest; and the fundamental means of stretching is incomplete rhythm.

In the Wagner and Chopin excerpts, we have been examining the feelings associated with anacruses, accents, and afterbeats, by analyzing cases in which each of these aspects of rhythmic grouping is prominent either because of having been stretched on the primary level or because of being observable on higher architectonic levels. We have considered each of these things—anacrusis, accent, and afterbeats—as phases of movement: movement toward a goal, goal of movement, and subsidence of movement. We have described the feelings associated with these phases of movement as varieties of tension and release considered to be located somewhere between the "lyric" and "dramatic" poles.

The agitated mobility of the upbeats in the Wagner is succeeded by the dramatic mobility of the accents, and the upbeats themselves are increased in their dramatic tension by their echoing afterbeats. Against this we may cite the serene tension, the calm movement, of the anacruses in the Chopin Prelude, the calm, releasing effect of arrival at a goal of motion in measure 9 of the first movement of the "Jupiter" Symphony, and the characterizing mixture of lyrical afterbeats with the dramatic melodic rhythm—dramatic because of the conflict—in the Chopin Etude.

We have also examined some relationships between rhythm and dynamics: the "normal" dynamics of the Prelude; the characterizing, dramatic dynamics of the Etude; the unexpected-expected dynamics of the Wagner, with their sense of delayed arrival.

AN ACCENTED REST

We now turn to a case in which the relationships among the various factors studied so far have such a startling result in the rhythm as to make it at the least rare, and possibly unique. The example is the climax of the development section in the first movement of Beethoven's "Eroica" Symphony (Example 137).

Just before the passage to be discussed, two previously established rhythms have come together (Example 138). The first of these (*a*), initially heard in measures 45 ff., has an anacrusis made heavy because of temporal relationship; the second (*b*), initially heard in measures 25 ff., has an even heavier anacrusis because of its characteristic sforzandi. These two rhythms have established for the passage in question a prior organization—an end-accented one. But, when we get to measure 272, the grouping is ambiguous: is it beginning-accented or end-accented? The accent which previously followed the anacrusis (cf. Example 138*b*) now occurs in a part of the texture separated from the part in which the anacrusis appears, and the separation makes the expected end-accented grouping insecure—more accurately, vividly potential—with the result that the accents in the bass feel like fresh beginnings of incompleted rhythms, and the whole passage up to measure 280 becomes an anacrusis of almost unbearable tension. This effect is heavily supported by the harmonic movement: the diminished-seventh chord which is mobile (but where is it going?); the six-four chord which is non-harmonic; and the clangorous seventh chord of measures 276–79 the function of which is analyzable only in retrospect, when we reach the dominant of E minor in measure 280.

EXAMPLE 137

EXAMPLE 138

And what does this anacrusis lead up to? Of all things, to a rest—to an accent, that is, which is unheard. It is this rest, this silence, which has been marked for consciousness by the movement in the preceding measures. So intense is that movement that this accent is expected to be powerfully stressed. The first beat of measure 280 must be the loudest silence in musical literature; one might say that it is so unbearably loud as to be inaudible. This powerful accent then rebounds in the repeated string chords, decrescendo, of measures 280–83, as an anacrusis to the E minor triad in measure 284. Thereupon we hear a regular, balanced, antecedent-consequent theme in, of course, an iambic grouping.

In this passage we may observe again that incomplete rhythm can help create a long, intense anacrusis, and that ambiguity of harmony is a factor in building tension; also that a mobile goal of movement (the first beat of measure 280) re-requires time before it is succeeded by its goal of resolution, if it has been led up to

EXAMPLE 139

by a long anacrusis. We may further observe here that the place where the most stressed accent is expected is a rest, but that the accent, the goal of movement, with the strongest attractive power in the passage (indeed, in the development section up to this point) is a piano triad (the E minor triad on the first beat of measure 284).

The piano triad, which completes the rhythm in this passage, should be differentiated from the piano chord in measure 50 of the *Tristan* excerpt. There, the piano accent turned into a fresh beginning of the same rhythm; here, after completion of the rhythm, a new one is introduced. It should never have astounded anybody that the new rhythm is of a new theme: after the intense feeling of going some place that arises from measures 272–83 (and what precedes them), where could one possibly go unless it be to a place where one has not yet been? This feeling of going some place, followed by the feeling of *being* some place (measures 284–88), gives one a vivid example of the rhythmic side of the differentiation of passages according to function, which is such an important aspect of formal progression in music.

It will no doubt have occurred to the reader that the movement from which Example 137 is excerpted ends with almost the same rhythm, but fully expressed in sound (Example 139). But this satisfies us by connecting in retrospect with the electrifying climax in the development section; it is not foreseen. For the rhythm of Example 137 is complete; it requires nothing further to make it seem finished. It is a moment of crisis, tonal and rhythmic, in the piece. But the crisis is over with the entrance of the E minor theme. The end of the movement, on the other hand, is a moment of triumph. Clarity has replaced confusion. Instead of the subsidence of measures 280–83 we have the climbing anacrusis of measures 685–88. What was broken has now become positive. That is, within what is fundamentally the same rhythm, we have two diametrically opposed characters. Again, the connection between the two passages is one discovered in retrospect— and it is one of the most brilliant strokes in the piece; but there was no prospect that the defeat of the one passage would turn into the victory of the other.

SUMMARY EXAMPLE

Finally, in order to make clear by way of summary the most important principles applied in this chapter, let us revert briefly to a previous example, the Minuet from Haydn's "London" Symphony (Example 140). In the individual

EXAMPLE 140

rhythmic impulse, the peculiar shape of the grouping has, as we have seen, certain aspects, among them accent, stress, tension, and their opposites. Although these aspects are analytically separable, the various notes of the impulse are not separable without destroying the quality of the shape as a whole.

This quality is of a completed rhythmic, melodic, and usually harmonic movement which either implies further such movements or constitutes an end of them. The sense of melodic and harmonic movement is a function of the relative mobility of individual notes and combinations thereof peculiar to the particular style.

Each impulse has not only a rhythmic shape with its center of gravity, its accent, but also a melodic shape with its center, its main note or melodic goal, and in non-monophonic music a harmonic shape with its center upon a main chord. Each of these centers may be on its own scale of relative mobility, and they frequently do not coincide in time. But the melodic and harmonic aspects of the impulse are part of its rhythmic shape.

As we move from the individual impulse to groups of impulses, to larger rhythms, the importance of melody and harmony in establishing the rhythmic feeling becomes even more clear.

Consider the second foot on the primary level in Example 140. The first foot has already established the rhythmic norm and the meter, and we know that the second foot is a middle-accented grouping with a stressed upbeat. The foot begins with an anacrusis (B) which moves toward the accented note (A) which, in turn, is followed by an echo or afterbeat falling away from the accent. Within the foot itself, the anacrusis is melodically and harmonically mobile and the accent and afterbeat are static. If we change the foot to read as in Example 141*b* we still have a middle-accented rhythm as in the original (*a*), but the kind of movement is different because the anacrusis is of a special kind, an anticipation, the accented note and chord are mobile, and the final afterbeat is their resolution; accent, and melodic and harmonic goals of movement, do not coincide. Or change the foot to read as in *c*, and melodic center, harmonic center, and accent all occur at different times.

EXAMPLE 141

In all cases, the A, whether accented or not, is the melodic center of gravity, the D major triad the harmonic, and the second note the rhythmic. Notice that, in *a*, mobility of melody and harmony coincides with the stressed upbeat, and accent and afterbeat are static; in *b*, mobility of melody and harmony coincides with stressed upbeat and with accent, but the afterbeat is static; in *c*, melody is static throughout, mobility of harmony coincides with stressed upbeat and with accent, and the afterbeat is static; in *d*, mobility of melody and harmony combines with upbeat but is separated from stress, which occurs on the accent, and the afterbeat is static; finally, in *e*, there is what one might call a crescendo of mobility—anticipation followed by accent—independent of stress. The reader is advised to consider very carefully the changes of character which result from these minute changes in the relative positions of stress, melodic mobility and goal, and harmonic mobility and goal. In each case, the foot is an amphibrach, but how different these amphibrachs are!

Let us revert to Example 140. The A, though melodically static within the second foot, is mobile after the foot has been completed and has become part of a series of feet. Indeed, the mobility of the A, from a higher standpoint, has been made clear within the first foot. In retrospect, after the first four measures are over, what has been accomplished melodically? Two things: first, the melody has gone easily up the tonic arpeggio from D to A and remained there; second, the descending anacrusis of the fourth foot has set up the most likely direction of melodic continuation, namely, downward. We expect movement downward from the A to occur in what follows. And it does in the next four measures.

Because of the feeling of implied movement toward something, followed by the feeling that the goal of that movement is being reached, the first four measures are an anacrusis to the second four and the first eight measures have the rhythmic shape of an iamb on the third level. On the second level there is also a definite rhythmic shape within the second four measures, that of an anapest.

Now, although the general sense of tension—what one might call the feeling tone—is not very high in this piece, the first four measures have a relatively high tension, because of the feeling of suspended but anticipatory motion which arises from the initial arpeggio followed by the centering of motion upon A and the tonic triad. This is subtle tension, when compared with that which arises from measures 67–70 of the *Tristan* excerpt, but it is there. And the melodic and harmonic movement of measures 5–8 of the Minuet satisfies us by completing the anticipated movement.

The lengths of the rhythmic groups on higher architectonic levels in this piece —two measures, four measures, and eight measures—are not accidental. In most, perhaps all, styles there are lengths of time in which the various significant segments of the music tend normally to take shape as rhythmic groups, and groups of groups. This fact is an aspect of form. And it is to form and matters connected with it, and their relationship to rhythm, that we turn in the next chapter.

EXERCISES

I

A. Analyze Mozart's "Jupiter" Symphony, first movement, measures 1–19, on all architectonic levels. What changes occur in rhythmic organization as a result of changes in melodic movement, harmony, orchestration, and other musical elements?

B. Analyze measures 78–93 of the first movement of Schubert's C Major Symphony. Write a brief essay discussing the rhythmic structure of this passage and its relationship to the other elements of music.

C. Make a rhythmic analysis on all architectonic levels (including the subprimary) of measures 1–25 (first beat) of the first movement of Bruckner's Symphony No. 7. Write an essay discussing the anacruses on various architectonic levels in this passage. What must be done in performance to insure that these anacruses will be heard as such? For instance, what would happen if the grouping on the primary level at the beginning were interpreted thus:

D. Analyze measures 1–36 of "Grillen" from Schumann's *Fantasiestücke*. In an essay discuss the conflict of accents between voices in measures 1–24 and the opposition of different rhythmic organizations in measures 25–36. In what ways does the rhythmic organization affect the character of the piece? What role does the title of this piece play in your interpretation of these rhythms?

E. Analyze measures 258 (last beat) through 317 of the first movement of Tchaikovsky's Symphony No. 6. Write an essay comparing this passage with those from the "Eroica" Symphony and *Tristan und Isolde* analyzed in this chapter.

II. Using the first eight measures of Brahms's Intermezzo Op. 116 No. 6 as a model, compose a series of variants which, though involving changes in melody, harmony, and dynamics (including stress), do not alter the rhythm of the primary level. Be prepared to discuss in class the effect of these changes upon the character of each variant.

VI

RHYTHM, CONTINUITY, AND FORM

Let us say that a musical theme is articulated into three parts, two measures, two measures, and four measures in length, respectively. We are talking about the phrasing of the theme. Are we also talking about rhythm? Or let us say that a whole piece or movement is articulated into four parts which, traditionally, we label *A A B A*. We are talking about the form of the piece or movement. Are we also talking about rhythm?

RHYTHM, FORM, AND MORPHOLOGICAL LENGTHS

In order to answer these questions, the reader is asked (for the last time in this book) to begin by examining a traditional tune—"Au clair de la lune" (Example 142). It is on the second architectonic level that the structural pattern of the

EXAMPLE 142

tune is established. The opening motive is two measures long. The second motive, which is clearly related to the first and complements it, serves to confirm the two-measure length as the unit of organization. And so on throughout. Structural lengths of time such as these will be called "morphological lengths."

Just as there are hierarchies of rhythm in a piece, so are there hierarchies of morphological length. The movement away from the G in measure 1 of our tune imparts a melodic mobility which, combined with the greater length of the accented B in measure 2, causes the first two measures to group as an iamb. But this iamb ends on the mobile note A and thereby assumes the character of an anacrusis on the third level. The two two-measure lengths become a four-measure length. So far, then, in talking about phrasing we are also talking about rhythm. For 2 + 2 = 4 here means that on the third architectonic level there

144

is an iamb. But notice that the phrasing $2 + 2 = 4$ does not necessarily imply an end-accented grouping; it could just as well be associated with a beginning-accented one (see Example 90, level 3); or, as we shall see (in Examples 143 and 144*b*), with the upbeats of a longer, anapestic one.

The first four measures of our tune are rhythmically and melodically complete, or "closed off." We anticipate that more music is to come, simply because tunes in our culture do not tend to be this short. But we have no notion of how the tune will continue except for the vague one that there will probably be some obvious connection between what we have heard and what we are about to hear and except for the clearer one that the already established morphological lengths, $2 + 2 = 4$, are likely to continue.

The actual continuation, of course, is a mere repetition, emphasizing the closed-off quality of the first four measures by means of an echo. In retrospect, therefore, the rhythmic shape of the first eight measures is that of a trochee on the fourth level. In this case, $4 + 4 = 8$ means a beginning-accented rhythm. But it will be unnecessary here, certainly, to go through the steps of showing that measures 9–16 are also, morphologically, $2 + 2 = 4$, $4 + 4 = 8$, and that $4 + 4 = 8$ means, in *this* case, an end-accented rhythm.

Let us imagine that we are hearing "Au clair de la lune" for the first time, and that we have arrived at the end of the first eight measures. What do we *know* about the rest of the tune, and what do we *feel* about the rest of the tune?

We must pause here and examine the difference between knowledge and feeling in this sort of situation. Think, for example, of the usual minuet and trio of the classical symphony. When we reach the end of the minuet, we know that we are about to hear the trio, unless the composer is playing tricks on us. But the minuet is closed off. The melodic, harmonic, and rhythmic issues which have been raised during the course of the minuet have been resolved. There is no demand for more music. That is, there is no feeling that the music has to go on in order to arrive at a goal toward which it has been pressing. There is simply the knowledge that more (and different) music is about to follow. If, as in Mozart's Quintet in G Minor, the trio turns out to be melodically connected to the minuet, we are surprised.

Now, at the end of measure 8 in "Au clair de la lune," we know, for stylistic reasons, that we are almost certainly hearing a tune in the form *A A B A*, but there is no feeling that the melody must move on in *B* to a particular goal. The tune has no mobility left in it at this point. The situation is similar to that at the end of measure 2 in the first movement of the "Jupiter" Symphony: on the highest architectonic level perceptible at that point, nothing has yet happened in the music. We know that something will happen, that movement will occur, but there is no direction of movement established which causes us to feel that something particular *must* occur.

When we arrive at the end of measure 12 in our tune, however, we not only know that *A* is going to be repeated; we also feel that it has to be. This is another way of saying that measures 9–12 are an anacrusis to a particular accent or goal.

In this case, then, the form *A A B A* is not one rhythm but two. Or, in terms of morphological lengths, (4 + 4 = 8) + (4 + 4 = 8) is two rhythms; and the rhythms are different: the first is a trochee and the second is an iamb. But the *whole* tune is not a rhythm, though it is a form. In another case, the form *A A B A* might well be one rhythm (see Example 115) and then rhythm and form would be the same thing. Whether or not this occurs depends upon the actual movement and implications of movement in the music.

For instance, if we rewrite the tune as in Example 143, there is established on the fourth architectonic level, by the end of measure 8, a definite melodic movement from G to A (secondarily from B to C) which we feel must continue to B

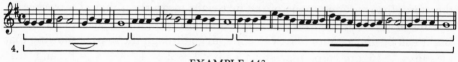

EXAMPLE 143

(and D) and return to G in order to form a complete group. At the end of measure 8 of this version, we feel more than know; we are in a group rather than at the end of a part. *A A B A* is a rhythm. And 4 + 4 + (4 + 4 = 8) is both a form *and* a rhythm.

We must conclude that a form *may* be a rhythm, but that no form is *necessarily* a rhythm. Alfred Lorenz, who contributed more than one valuable tool for musical analysis, maintained that form was macro-rhythm (*Grossrhythmik*).[1] It is often the case with important insights into the nature of music that one can easily go astray by denying their validity because they are found not to be universally true. It is much more likely that they are part of an as yet undiscovered, more comprehensive truth. A form often is a rhythm, and it is most certainly stultifying to think of form as a static thing. It is not too much to say that this book would not have been what it is without Lorenz, in spite of the fact that his conclusions are not accepted *in toto*. Incidentally, this book, or any book that deals with melodic analysis, has been influenced by Heinrich Schenker.[2] One does not have to accept a whole gospel in order to learn from it. It is probably very rarely, if ever, true that a method of musical analysis is wholly wrong. It is often true that it simply goes too far.

We may also tentatively conclude that morphological lengths tend to be symmetrical: that, for example, two measures of anacrusis will tend to be followed by two measures of accent in an iambic rhythm; or that two two-measure anacruses will tend to be followed by four measures of accent in an anapestic

[1] *Das Geheimnis der Form bei Richard Wagner* (Berlin: Max Hesses Verlag, 1924), Vol. I.

[2] *Der freie Satz*, ed. and rev. Oswald Jonas (Vienna: Universal Edition, 1956).

rhythm. But we have no right—at least as yet—to conclude with Riemann[3] that any other kind of phrasing implies a lengthening, a compression, or a suppression of symmetrical phrasing in morphological lengths of powers of two. Here is another case in which it is far too easy to throw out the baby with the bath water. For what Riemann observed was the *norm* in the phrasing of that kind of music the chief ancestor of which is the song and dance. To see that this is the case, all that one has to do is to suppress measures 9–10 in Example 142, or measures 10–11 in Example 143; the result is not antimusical, but it is felt immediately to be "odd" or "special." Of course, Riemann felt also that all groupings by measures were end-accented, and his readers are often disturbed by the contortions he is at times forced to go through in order to make end-accented rhythms; yet end-accented rhythm on the measure level is certainly more common than not, especially at the end of a piece.

Suppose that we change the first four measures of the tune into the first four measures of Example 144*a*. We now have an anacrusis demanding, normally,

EXAMPLE 144

four more measures to close off the larger grouping, and the form *A A'* becomes iambic. Or suppose that, as in Example 144*b*, we repeat the first four measures. We should have a 4 + 4 anacrusis requiring a melodic continuation—an accented phrase—eight measures long, if the morphological lengths are to remain normal; here, the *lengths*, 4 + 4 + (4 + 4 = 8), and the *form*, *A A B*, are in *rhythm* an anapest.

Form, then, may coincide with and *be* a rhythm, or it may not. And in the kind of music represented by our tune, morphological lengths are normally symmetrical: that is, the length of an anacrusis or of an afterbeat is normally equal to the length of an accent, on the highest level.

CONTINUITY AND FORM

Now form is one kind of continuity. Continuity in music is the sense of connection between any one point of time in a piece and the next point of time. Put in

[3] Hugo Riemann, *System der musikalishen Rhythmik und Metrik* (Leipzig: Breitkopf und Härtel, 1903).

a more general way, if, while listening to a piece, you feel that there is going to be more music than you have already heard, the piece has continuity. Continuity exists on all architectonic levels, and it arises now from melodic or harmonic mobility, now from rhythm, now from form, and often from a combination of some or all of these.

In Example 142, the continuity between the two halves of the tune arises from form only. In Example 143, the continuity between the two halves arises from melodic and harmonic mobility, from form (including its aspect of morphological lengths), and from the resulting rhythm. The same thing is true of both *a* and *b* in Example 144. But this is to speak of "Au clair de la lune" and the distortions of it only from the highest architectonic level.

On lower levels, the temporary cessations of movement represented by the whole-notes are quite prominent. That is, none of these tunes has strong *immediate* continuity, as we may call it; many pulses are suppressed.

Suppose that we alter the tune as in Example 145 in order to give it more

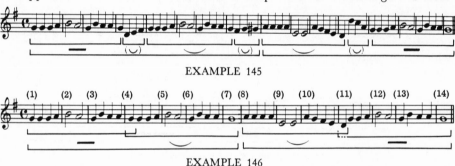

EXAMPLE 145

EXAMPLE 146

obvious and immediate continuity. The results may be surprising, inasmuch as the inserted "links" have no real effect on the phrase rhythm. They seem to be parenthetical (as indicated in the analysis). The listener feels just as strongly as he did while listening to the original tune that the first phrase ends on G, that the second begins and ends on G, and so on. Continuity is analytically separate from phrase rhythm, though the two may coincide.

An even more surprising effect results from overlapping phrases, as has been done in two cases in Example 146. Here, the first G in measure 4 is simultaneously the end of the first phrase and the beginning of the second. Paradoxically, movement starts and stops in one note. Notice, however, that the morphological lengths are really altered: the sense of entering a new length of time at the beginning of measure 4 is sufficiently strong that we feel the first seven measures to be really the sum of 3 + 4 rather than 4 + 4 with one measure in common.

The case in measure 11 is somewhat different. Here, one phrase ends on D (but that note is allowed insufficient time) and the next starts on G in such a way that its beginning seems to have been omitted. Immediate continuity has been obtained at the price of being ludicrous. And the mind is confused about the phrasing, as it was not in measure 4. This is a fake overlapping. Does seven result here from $3\frac{1}{4} + 3\frac{3}{4}$? What happens in measure 4, however, is a familiar occurrence.

We have tried both links and overlappings as means of increasing immediate continuity and have seen that they do not really affect rhythm, except insofar as overlappings affect morphological lengths. But suppose we try interrupting continuity. Will this affect rhythm?

A case of interrupted continuity that comes readily to mind is found in the classical concerto, in which the resolution of a I_4^6 chord onto a V chord may be delayed for several minutes by the insertion of a cadenza. The effect of this kind of interruption (and of similar kinds) is perhaps even more surprising than are the effects of links and overlappings. For two things happen. First, suspense results, and suspense intensifies whatever continuity there may be. It may be several seconds after the lightning flash that the sound of thunder reaches our ears, but when we see the lightning we know the thunder will follow. Second, there is a certain unreality about the interruption. It is not part of the "real" piece, which will resume as though nothing had happened whenever it is allowed to. In one sense, of course, the cadenza is part of the piece because we expect it to be there; in another very real sense, however, it is not. There are somewhat analogous cases in both art and literature. A painting is supposed to have a frame; the frame is not part of the painting—but it is. A story with a frame—for example, a play within a play or a novel with a flashback—includes and does not include the frame. Extraneous comic interludes are and are not parts of a serious play. A ballet in an opera does and does not belong to that opera. And so on.

We may test this by performing a final operation on "Au clair de la lune" (Example 147). Here two insertions have been made.

Notice first, in Example 147a, the effect of resuming in measure 8 an activity which stopped in measure 4. We still relate, both melodically and rhythmically, measures 8–11 to measures 1–4. In fact, we group them together in spite of intervening measures. Furthermore, we are more aware of morphological length in the real tune than we are in the interruption, which in effect is something like a composed fermata, a delay. And we may say the same thing of measures 12–21. Our sense of grouping has not fundamentally altered; it is only that delay has been introduced. This delay may be easily increased. For instance, substitute the three measures in *b* for measures 16–17 in *a*. Or take the last note of *b* and add a coloratura cadenza to it before resuming the tune at measure 18.

Then notice that no matter what may be the case on the lowest architectonic levels, on the highest level the insertions *do not group*. There is no accent. Everything is anacrusis. There is no real rhythm. The insertions in the example are in-complete rhythms. The reader may feel that the last three notes in measure 7 (or the corresponding passages in Example 145) find their accent on the first note of the next measure. This may be true on the subprimary level—perhaps even on the primary one—but certainly on the highest level there is no group of which any of these insertions is a part. This is precisely because they *are* insertions. They interrupt a group, the character of which has already been established. In Ex-ample 147*a*, for instance, we know that measures 1–4 will be followed by an afterbeat, not by another accent, which measures 8–11 would become if the interruption were an anacrusis to them; and we know that the anacrusis of measures 12–15 will be followed by the accent of measures 18–21—this for formal

EXAMPLE 147

reasons—not by another anacrusis, which would make the whole shape of measures 12–21 that of an anapest, and the shape of those measures is clearly not that; the difference in motivic material between measures 12–15 and measures 16–17, as well as the difference in length, rule it out. Simplicity favors thinking of these incomplete rhythms as composed fermatas, as delays.

It may be objected that because our tune is a familiar one, insertions cannot help being obvious as such. Indeed, many a well-known tune, such as "Alouette" or "The Twelve Days of Christmas," actually starts as a pair of phrases between which longer and longer insertions are made as the song goes on and we can hardly think of these insertions as being parts of the tune, though they are parts of the song. Let the reader think of the first movement of Beethoven's Symphony No. 7. Does he not feel that the real beginning of the exposition occurs only when he hears the main theme, and that the reiterated E's (and, later, C-sharps and A's) are introductory and are not in the same sense part of the piece? We shall have an opportunity later on in this chapter to examine incomplete rhythm more carefully.

Before we leave our tune, one more thing about it needs to be pointed out. There are only two (very similar) rhythmic motives in it, and each of them is exactly two measures in length. Repetition of these motives, then, establishes and maintains meter. The morphological lengths are measured by these motives. Not all music has this coincidence between length of motive and morphological length. But before we analyze a piece in which this fact is demonstrated, let us revert to Chopin's Prelude in E-flat in order to examine within a larger scope the interrelationships among rhythm, continuity, and form.[4]

In the discussion of this piece, measures 1–16 will be referred to as *A*, measures 17–32 as *B*, measures 33–49 as *A'*, and the rest of the piece as the "coda."

As is so often true of pieces with a powerful homogeneity of character and thematic material, the immediate continuity of the Prelude is high. The continuity of the triplet figure on the subprimary rhythmic level is not broken until the last three measures, except in measure 32, where strong continuity is provided by the harmony; on the third beat of that measure there is a dominant which demands movement to the tonic which begins measure 33. Furthermore, the rest at that point serves to emphasize the impending return of *A* as *A'*, an event we have been anticipating since *A* closed in the dominant key in measure 16.

The rhythm on the primary level also provides continuity. It consists characteristically of stretched amphibrachs which fit the meter. That is, all the groups start on the third beat and end on the second. The feminine ending of this characteristic rhythm makes it look ahead to an end-accented rhythm which does not occur until the cadence of *A'* (measure 49), so that there is constant forward motion in the rhythm. (The transition from middle-accented to end-accented rhythm is made by means of pivoting, as can be seen by consulting the analysis of measures 45–49, primary level.)

The mobility of melody and harmony is high. There is no authentic cadence in E-flat until the end of *A'*, where, also for the first time, the melody comes to rest on the tonic.

The form is one which, along with the factors already mentioned, provides for continuity of movement. It is a favorite with Chopin (and, among others, with Brahms), and combines the principles of ternary structure with those of binary. The initial section (*A*) is not closed off tonally as it is in the normal ternary form, but instead modulates, as in the antecedent of a binary form. The intervention of a contrasting section (*B*), which delays the expected consequent, insures formal continuity.

[4] The Prelude is printed on pp. 185–87.

In this piece, *B* is so like *A* in motive that the form *A BA'*—were there no coda—would become a large iamb the accent of which was itself an iamb. But by the end of *A'* we are aware of another factor which demands the continuation into a coda. This factor is the one of morphological lengths.

In spite of the slightly agitated air of measures 29–32, brought about by the metric conflict which almost comes to the surface in that passage, the piece is one of great serenity, and it demands a sense of balance. No disproportion would fit the mood. The anacrusis of measures 1–16 (see analysis below) is too short for the accent of measures 17–49. To end at measure 49, the transition from middle-accented to end-accented rhythm having just been made, would be too abrupt. In a piece with a different character, abruptness or disproportion or both might have been desirable, but not here. Therefore, more time is needed to make the elements of unaccent balance those of accent in length. There is a coda, and the form becomes an amphibrach (on the fourth rhythmic level) the accent of which is an iamb.

A   BA'   Coda

4.

In the coda, the two rhythms on the primary level are combined by pivoting. And, as a coda to the coda, measures 66–69 do for the end-accented rhythm something like what measures 29–32 did for the middle-accented one, except that they do it in tranquillo, with the harmony tied down to the tonic and ending with a diminuendo. The coda's coda has in turn a coda, the two chords of measures 70–71.

The phrasing, as set forth in the following table in terms of morphological lengths, should be compared with the analysis under the score, because such a comparison will make quite clear the interconnection among form, rhythm, and continuity, as exemplified in this piece.

A	$4(3+1)+2+2=8$
	$4(3+1)+4 \quad =8$
B	$2+2+4=8$
	$2+2+4=8$
A'	$4(3+1)+2+2=8$
	4 closely linked with $4(+)=8(+)$
Coda	$2+2+4=8$
	$2+2+4=8$
	4
	2

It is not strange that the rhythms of *A* and *A'* should be so much alike, but it is interesting that those of *B* and the coda are. *B* is a passage of tonal movement and of upward melodic striving; the coda stays close to home tonally and has the melodic function of again bringing the melody down to the tonic. The passage in measures 66–69 has already been compared with the one in measures 29–32. The relationship between the first sixteen measures of the coda and *B* is similar: compared with *B*, the coda is tranquillo; it is a genuine afterbeat.

In this piece rhythm and meter are almost always at one, as they always are in "Au clair de la lune." Again, rhythmic groups and morphological lengths coincide. In this case rhythm measures, except in the passage during which the change of rhythm occurs (measures 45–49). And the effects of melody, harmony, and form can all be made subject to the summarizing influence of rhythmic analysis.

THEMES, NON-THEMES, AND CONTINUITY

But suppose rhythms are more varied? Suppose the lengths of the groups are not compatible with the number of pulses in a measure? How will phrasing and other aspects of form fit with rhythm then?

We have dealt with a simple tune, and then with a relatively simple piece. We now turn to the first movement of Beethoven's Symphony No. 8, in order to observe in the exposition of that movement the various factors that have so far been interrelated and to see them all in a different light. Before going on we must firmly establish a difference in formal conception between a work such as the Chopin Prelude in E-flat and a movement such as the one by Beethoven, part of which we are about to consider.

The difference hinges upon the notion vaguely expressed by the word "theme." In conformity with what appears to be the most common practice, "theme" will be used here to mean a musical idea sufficiently complete in itself that if it were removed from its surroundings it would make sense as an individual, small piece. Of course, the kind of sense a theme would make when heard out of context is not identical with the kind of sense it makes in context; the point is that a theme can be viewed as a diminutive but complete piece. Thus, a fugue subject is not a theme; a motive such as the first four notes of Beethoven's Symphony No. 5 is not a theme; and so on. The fugue subject, the motive, and the like, are not lacking in shape—they are recognizable in their individuality—but one cannot think of them as little pieces which happen to be imbedded in larger pieces. They are more like seeds of pieces.

To avoid misunderstanding, it should be pointed out that there is such a thing as an incomplete theme. Think, for example, of how Mozart's familiar Symphony in G Minor begins. We first hear half a theme, a passage ending with a strong semi-cadence. This half is an "antecedent," and we anticipate a "consequent" which will close on the tonic and complete the theme. But no sooner has the anticipated consequent started than it is deflected from G minor to B-flat major; new material is introduced, and the theme is never finished. And there are other varieties of "near-themes," as we might call them. We shall meet with one shortly.

Now, the Prelude does not *have* a theme; rather, it *is* a theme (or, if one insists, a theme plus a coda). The first movement of Symphony No. 8 contains themes. It also contains passages which are not themes or parts of themes. It is everywhere motivic, but it is not everywhere thematic. Let us first investigate the rhythmic consequences of these facts.

The movement begins (1–12)[5] with a theme in three phrases. The first phrase is an antecedent which is incompletely complemented by the second. The movement from tonic harmony to dominant in the first is answered by a movement from dominant to tonic in the second, but the sharp end-accented cadence (4) is in strong contrast with the gentle middle-accented one (8). The third phrase (9–12) is the real consequent of the first (cf. 190–97). The movement, then, begins with a twelve-measure accent, for a theme (or a series of themes) is a place of arrival or of departure, a goal of motion or a home base away from which motion is about to occur.

The next phrase (13–20) is also a theme—this time with an anapestic shape. But it is of a different kind. It has an affirmative, conclusive function, like a codetta. It is melodically centered on the tonic, F, and its sequence of harmonies (I–IV[6]–II$_5^6$–V–I) is cadential. It is an afterbeat of the opening theme. Imagine it repeated without change and followed by two more measures, each with a tonic triad on its first beat. Does it not sound like the end of a section or of a movement? It does start to repeat (21 ff.) but soon breaks down into fragments on a harmony without specific direction. The F–A-flat–B-flat–D chord is not a dominant of E-flat in this uncompromisingly "F-ish" context. It is a mobile chord without specific direction. The afterbeat theme has turned into an upbeat passage—but an upbeat to what? When the harmony moves to a dominant of D (34), the goal of movement is in part clear. It is something in D. The mode is a surprise (38), for the expected mode was minor. In retrospect, the A-flat in the harmony of the previous passage (24–33) is interpreted as a G-sharp in an augmented-sixth chord.

The whole section from the end of the opening theme down to the entrance of D major begins as a theme but continues, through fragmentation, as a non-theme; it begins as an afterbeat but becomes an upbeat. The upbeat, of course, we expect will lead to an accent—in other words, to a theme. And, as the violins start out in D major (38–41), a theme is what we are apparently hearing. It is not a theme for long, however, because its tonality is unstable. The harmony is on the

---

[5] In this discussion, the numbers in parentheses refer to measures. The score is printed on pp. 188 ff.

move from D to C (42–45), in which key the melody starts to repeat. The accent which we thought we had reached has turned into an anacrusis.

Notice the play with the appearance and the reality of theme so far. The movement begins with a real theme, a sport (we might say) in the antecedent-consequent family. It continues with what appears to be a codetta theme of the self-repeating family. The deflected repeat, however, causes the appearance to break down and reveal the anacrustic reality. Next comes another apparent theme—again of the antecedent-consequent family—which, in its turn, is revealed as an anacrusis.

We now reach a passage which is non-thematic from the start (52–69). It is clearly a passage of harmonic movement with the function of establishing the key of C major. In rhythmic terms, it is an anacrusis to a C major accent. And this time, the theme *is* a theme (70–90), an accent.

This theme is of the self-repeating family, with each half containing sharp contrast. It will pass the test of standing on its own feet if removed from its context, although its feet will not be very stable. This is because of the violent nature of the contrast here, a contrast in dynamics, in melody, and especially in meter. The metric contrast would let us know, if we heard this theme out of context, that it is of some later-in-the-piece variety. It could not begin a movement. In context, however, it is definitely stable; it is a place, a goal of motion, an accent.

Like the opening one, this theme has an afterbeat or codetta (90–103). The codetta is melodically allied to the theme. Compare the movement E–D, F–E of the theme (70–71 and 80–81) with the same fundamental movement (in different rhythm) of the codetta (90–92). The by now familiar process of change into an anacrusis occurs here too. It is the added B-flat in measure 103 which makes this change definite. The conversion of the last four measures of the exposition (100–103) into an anacrusis has important consequences in the development section, as we shall see in the next chapter.

Broadly speaking, form in this exposition is an aspect of differentiation among passages according to function: theme, codetta, passage of movement, and the like. Rhythm follows function. The continuity which arises from a play with function is clear. We wish to hear themes, and our wish to hear them is guided by the force of tonality within the very generalized scheme of sonata form. But there is another important source of continuity here, and it is to this that we now turn.

What of morphological lengths? The opening theme falls within normal lengths, 4 + 4 + 4. The important word here is "within." For it may be said quite baldly at the start that themes are completed within morphological lengths but that non-themes are not, unless they have a coda function. The significance of this statement will become apparent as we go on.

The next theme (the codetta, or whatever one wishes to call it) is regularly constructed, 2 + 2 + 4, and so might be supposed to fall within its morphological lengths, but it does not. For while the first violins are playing the last note, F, of the opening theme (12), the second violins and violas are starting the accompaniment of the new theme. This new theme does not overlap melodically with the previous theme, since it does not begin until the next measure (13), but it does overlap in accompaniment. As this accompaniment begins (12), we cannot help feeling, quite simply, that something new has started. This new something is a morphological length.

The new morphological length (12–19) begins on an accent, the final one of the end-accented opening theme. The new theme (13–20) is end-accented on the measure level, as was the old. Therefore, the accents continue to fall on the even-numbered measures, but these measures become, starting at measure 12, the odd-numbered measures in the morphological length. This means that the *end* of the new theme (20) comes at the *beginning* of a new length, and a powerful kind of continuity has been established. The new theme cannot be completed within its own length, for its length overlaps the length established by the accompaniment. Notice the reinforcement of the beginning of a new length in measure 20 by means of the sustained wind chords and the drum rolls.

In short, an end-accented rhythm is combined with beginning-accented morphological lengths. This means that, no matter how conclusive the theme may sound in melody, harmony, and rhythm, the music will be pushed forward with great force by accompaniment and orchestration, because the end is at the same time a beginning.

This phenomenon can be profitably regarded as a metrical one. As was pointed out in chapter i,[6] meter exists on several levels, although the kind of notation in use at Beethoven's time limits the apparent number of levels. The passage we have been considering firmly establishes a duple meter on the measure-to-measure level. And we are shortly going to be made quite conscious of the fact that a measure may be reduced to the status of a beat.

For the sake of clarity, let us review the first twenty measures metrically on the measure-to-measure level. We begin with a rhythm which goes across the bar line of a 2 × ¾ meter: 2–1, 2–1, etc. The note F in measure 12 is, thus, on a downbeat. If the rhythm here is to behave in a normal fashion, as was the case in the Chopin piece, this F will be the end of something. But a new idea, the accompaniment in the second violins and violas, starts in a rhythm which stays within the bar lines: 1–2, 1–2, etc. Therefore, although the new melody (13–20) continues to move across the bar lines, it cannot come to an end, because the new accompaniment begins again.

Once the existence of meter on a higher level than that indicated by the time signature is clear, it is easy to notice the phenomenon which we shall call "reduction to meter"—the phenomenon, that is, of reducing a measure to the

[6] See pp. 4–5; also pp. 109–15.

status of a beat. This is observable in the passage starting in measure 28. In this passage each measure begins with an accented D, and these D's force themselves on the attention by their regular recurrence, so that one subconsciously counts them. If, for analytical purposes, we count them consciously, we do so as follows (28–33): *1* 2 3 4 *1* 2 (empty measure). Going on (34–38), we count *1* 2 3 4 *1* (beginning of D major "theme"). Notice that the measures as metric units are so well established that the end-accented rhythmic figure which is the motivic substance of the passage has lost its upbeat at the end of measure 33. This loss signalizes the beginning of a new morphological length, a new higher-level measure, at measure 34. The reader should test this statement by altering the music to read as in Example 148. He will see that the rhythmic figure is not

EXAMPLE 148

EXAMPLE 149

functioning as such at all; it is a mere unit in the real rhythm, which is proceeding on the measure level. More accurately, the *accent* of the rhythmic figure is the unit, the beat, in the real rhythm; a change of harmony and a shift to a new length such as we find at the beginning of measure 34 becomes awkwardly unclear by pretending, as in the example, that the end-accented motive is the primary rhythmic fact of the passage. The primary rhythm has no accent. It is an incomplete rhythm. This incompleteness is the rhythmic aspect of reduction to meter.

The importance of the measure as a metric unit in this piece is amply illustrated by the passage which follows (38–51). In the first part of this passage (Example 149) the rhythms begin by fitting the measures (as in the Chopin piece). But when we reach the high A (41) this is no longer the case. The A enters too soon. Indeed, from that point on through the next four measures, where do the rhythms begin and end? Although we cannot answer that question, we have no doubt at all about when the *measures* begin and end. Put in another way, the lengths in this passage are clear in terms of measures, but not in terms of first-level rhythms (except at the start). There is a tendency, not for *feet* to measure (as in the Chopin), but for *accents* (or measures) to measure. The reader may wish to observe the same thing in the opening theme of the movement. Congruence of rhythmic grouping on the primary level and measure is far less important here than in either of the two pieces considered earlier in this chapter.

The morphological lengths (38–45) appear to be $(1 + 1 + 2) + (1 + 1 + 2)$. In spite of the symmetry of these figures, however, the two sections they describe are quite different in function. The first section (through the E in 41) is a phrase, an antecedent phrase. It is part of a theme which is a member of the waltz family, part of some *alla tedesca* tune such as Example 150.

EXAMPLE 150

EXAMPLE 151

In this example the phrasing is normal and the shape is clear. The tune is, in fact, a theme. But in the actual music the entry of the high A (41) destroys the congruence of rhythmic group and meter, and, by pivoted groupings, extends the phrase through two more measures. The phrase becomes then, in lengths, really $1 + 1 + 2$—extended into two more. Now it ceases to be a proper phrase for a theme, not on account of its lopsided morphological lengths, but on account of its very morphology: it has no cadence. It moves by means of a two-measure link (44–45) into the next phrase, but it has become part of what might be called an ex-theme rather than a theme.

The extension initiated by the early-arriving high A (41) is important to the phrasing here, which is as follows: $(1 + 1 + 2 + 2 = 6) + 2$ (link). If the music is altered to make the A arrive politely, as in Example 151, two things happen: the *alla tedesca* character is emphasized by the regularity, and measures 42–45 altogether become a link. All the peculiar grace of the passage is gone.

The next passage (52–69) is, in morphological lengths, $3 + 4 + 2 + 4 + 4$. The motivic relationship among the parts is obvious. This passage is a non-

theme from the start and illustrates the statement that non-themes are not completed within morphological lengths unless they have a coda function.

Lest the reader suppose that the last phrase in the passage is really a five-
measure phrase which overlaps with the beginning of the ensuing theme, let him
add a measure between 69 and 70 containing octave C's on the first beat. The
effect is to prick the balloon of this powerful passage. Here again we have a reduction to meter. Take the last four measures (66–69) and count: *1* 2 3 4. This
means that the following *1*, the downbeat, is not the end of what has been going
on, but rather the beginning of something new, something beginning-accented.
Better yet, take the last eight measures (62–69) and omit measure 66. Now
count: *1* 2 3 4 *1* 2 3—the octave C's will be needed for completion, but the
passage will acquire a feminine ending where it obviously wants an accent.

The statement that non-themes are not completed within morphological
lengths (unless they have a coda function) can now be seen to mean that non-
themes cannot be completed at all when they function as anacruses. They are
anacruses to themes. When non-themes have a coda function, they are afterbeats
and can be closed off. See, for instance, the last two measures of the Prelude
discussed in this chapter, or the last two measures of Example 139.

EXAMPLE 152

As far as we have gone in the movement, morphological lengths have func-
tioned to provide continuity in three ways: by non-congruence with the phrase
rhythm (12 ff.); by reduction to meter, whether partial (23–28, 52–59) or complete (28–37, 60–69); and by extension and link (41–45). The rest of the exposition will provide little in the way of novel procedure.

The theme arrived at in measure 70 begins in ²⁄₄ meter with a phrase 1 + 1 +
(1 + 1 = 2). After the rebound on the third beat of measure 72, there is an
eight-measure phrase which genuinely overlaps with the beginning of the repetition at measure 80. When repeated, this eight-measure phrase is allowed to
complete itself on the first beat of measure 90, but there is no lack of rhythmic
continuity at this point for two reasons: first, the accompaniment (violas and
cellos) begins a new morphological length, just as it did in measure 12; second,
the new motive (Example 152a) has a different placement in the measure; it
begins on the second beat rather than on the third and therefore robs the previous
phrase of a beat.

The new placement of the rhythm in the measure continues, as in *b* of the example, until the rhythm is shorn of its afterbeat and is compressed into a $\frac{2}{4}$ meter (see *c*). The $\frac{2}{4}$ and $\frac{3}{4}$ meters are congruent on the first beat of measure 100, and the remaining four measures represent a reduction to meter. The morphological lengths of the codetta (90–103) are normally duple: $(1 + 1 = 2) + 4 + 4 + 4$.

There is a striking effect when the exposition is repeated. If we count the last four measures of the codetta (100–103), we get a meter (*1* 2 3 4) such as to bring a powerful accent on the first measure of the piece. But the opening theme is end-accented on the measure level, and the sudden shift brings an extraordinarily forceful accent to bear upon measure 2.

The continuity in this movement is less dependent upon low-level rhythm than was the case in the Chopin Prelude. But the continuity is not broken by such a thing as the pause in measures 32–33. It is even furthered by it because of the emphasis placed thereby on the role of the morphological lengths.

RHYTHM AND TEXTURE

In the Beethoven excerpt we have been considering, accompaniment is clearly important to continuity. What may be said generally of the rhythmic relationship among parts in a texture?

To begin with the obvious, accompaniment has the function of accompanying, and it will therefore normally be congruent rhythmically with the melody. In that kind of relatively homophonic texture which includes a striking accompaniment, the accompaniment not infrequently appears before the melody. More often than not it is rhythmically ambiguous until the melody appears, and even then it may be *in itself* incomplete rhythmically as a whole or in part.

In the third movement of Rimski-Korsakov's *Schéhérazade*, the alternating tune is introduced by its accompaniment (Example 153). The figure continues the previously established $\frac{6}{8}$ meter. It could just as well have established it— rhythm need not necessarily be either complete or unambiguous in order to establish meter. But we do not know how to group it as yet. The cellos and basses have only downbeats. The violas have only unaccents (except on the subprimary level); are these upbeats or afterbeats? The drum fits with the violas, but its part does not help to define the grouping. This accompaniment could support an end-accented rhythm or a beginning-accented one just as well as it supports the middle-accented one with which it does in fact go. When the middle-accented melodic motive enters in the clarinet, we group the accompaniment accordingly. The whole texture is now quite clear rhythmically, even though no one orchestral color in the accompaniment carries a complete rhythm. And it is clear on every architectonic level.

Not all textures, however, support so many architectonic levels of rhythm as do the pieces we have considered so far in this chapter. Although, as a whole, "Au clair de la lune" has two rhythms, the other two pieces can each be comprehended as a single rhythm. The Prelude, as we have seen, is a large middle-accented rhythm the accent of which is itself an iamb. The Beethoven move-

EXAMPLE 153

ment, on the highest level, is an anapest the accent of which is an amphibrach, as follows:

Exposition	Exposition repeated	Development	Recapitulation	Coda

(The anacrustic character of the development section in this movement will be considered in the next chapter.)

Now, these large rhythms associated with forms are possible because of clearly articulated phrasing associated with morphological lengths. A style which sets a premium on the immediate continuity derived from overlapping tends toward an almost constant pivoting of rhythms. This results in a continuity different in kind from that which we have seen displayed in the pieces so far considered in this chapter.

Such a style is that of most Bach fugues. In these, morphological lengths are

seldom important. Indeed, the measure itself is frequently of so little importance
as a unit that repeated rhythmic groupings are not always placed in the same
position with respect to the measure and this does not alter the effect, so long as
the relative position of weak and strong beats remains constant. In such cases,
counting by two's or by three's is more important than the number of two's or
three's to a measure.

At times, the relationship between subject and countersubject is the opposite
of the relationship between melody and accompaniment in the *Schéhérazade* example. That is, the rhythm of the subject itself may be incompleted or unclari-
fied, and the contrapuntal accompaniment provided by the countersubject may
be required to complete or clarify the rhythm.

EXAMPLE 154

For instance, in the Fugue in F-sharp Minor from Book II of Bach's *Well-
tempered Clavier*, the opening could appear to have the rhythm of Example 154a.
For stylistic reasons, we know this is incorrect, because it does not establish a
regular meter. Furthermore, we suspect from our previous experience that the
dotted quarters are suspended, and that the descending melodic motion is thus
brought about by resolving dissonances. With the entry of the answer, the two
voices together make the grouping quite clear. The rhythm is as we suspected
(*b*). Nothing in what follows, whenever the subject is present, alters this organization fundamentally.

In the Fugue in A Major from the same book, the rhythm of the subject alone
is more doubtful, and clarification (rather than confirmation) is necessary. The
subject appears to be grouped as in Example 155a. Again, we know because of
the meter that this is incorrect, but our suspicions are less firm than they were in

the previous case, for we can hardly anticipate the very individual upward-resolving tied notes. But by the middle of measure 3 the two voices together are beginning to group, and the music of the next measure establishes the meter clearly. With the entry of the third voice, we finally see that the subject is an intense anacrusis to its final note (Example 155*b*).

In both these cases, the counterpoint has created with the subject an unequivocal grouping by two means: completing the rhythms necessary to establish the meter, and clarifying the harmonic status of the various important notes in the subject. In the F-sharp minor fugue, the subject then becomes rhythmically and melodically finished and remains so. In the A major fugue, the subject retains its melodically tentative ending until the last measure of the piece, in which the melody is finally closed above a repetition of the end of the subject's rhythm in the middle voice (Example 155*c*). Notice that this fugue ends on an unequivocal downbeat which is not the first beat of the written measure.

EXAMPLE 155

In both fugues, the rhythms of the individual voices in the texture together issue in a rhythm which is without conflict. But conflicts of rhythm often occur in some contrapuntal styles.

For instance, in Beethoven's *Grosse Fuge*, the subject, as announced in measures 26–30, conflicts with the meter (Example 156). We suspect this (although the meter has not been established at this point) because of the nervous manner in which the performer, under the visual influence of the score, inevitably plays these measures. As the fugue proper begins (end of measure 30), we become cer-

EXAMPLE 156

tain that the subject has been syncopated, inasmuch as the countersubject establishes a very clear meter with which the subject does not "fit."

The conflict is, however, not merely a metric one. Each of the lines falls into two halves with an introduction, labeled *int.*, *I*, and *II* in the example. Not only do these halves not coincide for the obvious metric reason; the subject is melodically and harmonically slower than the countersubject. The harmonic implication of the countersubject is V of II–II, V–I (with a proper fugal twist to the dominant at the end) divided between the two halves; that of the subject is the same, but with more time allowed for the C minor portion (see brackets in Example 157). This harmonic implication is emphasized melodically by the simple antecedent-consequent symmetry of A-flat–G–F–E-flat, and G–F–E-flat–D (turning to F) in the countersubject, against the two-story line,

A-flat–G   A–B-flat (–A)

B-flat–B   B–C

in the subject, in which the movement initiated on the lower level (B-flat–B) has to wait for its continuation until the upper level has been activated (A-flat–G). This brings a strong accent to bear on the C in the subject (measure 34) which does not fit with the previous strong accent on the E-flat in the countersubject (measure 33). Also, it takes the subject longer to reach A-flat than it does the countersubject (see measure 32). These A-flats and their continuations are very prominent to the ear.

One result of this rhythmic conflict is that we have to hear in units of four measures: that is, with widely spaced rhythmic "consonances."[7] Another result of the conflict is stylistically interesting. The music of Beethoven is normally

EXAMPLE 157

articulated in clear morphological lengths and is normally homophonic in texture. We may expect, then, to hear the conflict resolved later in the piece by means of more frequent rhythmic consonances, resulting from harmonic clarification, and by means of simpler phrasing. In this version of the subject and this countersubject (Example 156), the conflict is resolved late in the coda (Example 158). In the following excerpt from the coda, we can hear, in order, the conflict (716–24) and its resolution (725–33).

In the passage of resolution, the odd-numbered measures are all accented in both contrapuntal parts (level 2). The phrasing is clear: 2 + 2 + 4, going on to the first beat of the next measure, because this is a non-theme with a coda function. And the kind of continuity is primarily that of homophonic music with rhythm on several architectonic levels.

The two Bach subjects and the Beethoven subject plus countersubject present what might be called "problems." In the case of the Bach subjects, these problems are promptly solved by the addition of counterpoint. The problem of Beethoven's material has to await solution until almost the end of the piece. But

---

[7] See p. 108, above.

in all three cases there is something about the initial rhythm which implies later developments, either proximate or remote.

In the final chapter, we shall consider four unlike cases of rhythmic development.

EXAMPLE 158

EXERCISES

I

A. Make an analysis of the rhythm of Beethoven's Bagatelle Op. 119, No. 1 and "Warum" from Schumann's *Fantasiestücke*, Op. 12.

B. Write an essay discussing the relationship among rhythm, form (including morphological lengths), and continuity in these pieces.

II. Find two pieces of homophonic music in which the accompaniment begins before the melody and the rhythmic structure of the melody serves to clarify the rhythm of the accompaniment. Be prepared to analyze and discuss these pieces in class.

III. Following the methods and procedures employed in the discussion of "Au clair de la lune," write a set of variants on folk tune "C" given in Exercise I at the end of chapter ii. Your variants should illustrate the following: overlapping, inserted anacruses, and rhythmic structures which are not complete within the morphological lengths. In each case write one or two sentences stating what you have done and how it has affected the rhythmic structure of the variant.

IV

A. Analyze the A-minor fugue from Book II of the *Well-tempered Clavier*. What is the rhythmic relationship between the first and second halves of the subject? Do the countersubjects enhance this relationship or oppose it? How is rhythmic continuity achieved in this fugue? Why is the end of the fugue rhythmically satisfactory?

B. Analyze the exposition of the G-minor fugue from Book II of the *Well-tempered Clavier*. How does the relationship among the voices serve to clarify the rhythmic structure of the subject?

V

A. Write a fugal exposition in three (or four) voices on the following subject by André Gedalge. Your counterpoint should be such that it clarifies the rhythmic structure of the subject.

B. Make a rhythmic analysis of your fugal exposition.

VII RHYTHMIC DEVELOP-MENT

It is obvious that the way in which a piece—or a section thereof—begins, has consequences for the way in which it continues. The beginning by no means determines the continuation, but it does set up certain possibilities of development. In this final chapter, we are concerned with four examples of these possibilities and their consequences. The reader is advised to have the complete score at hand for the study of each example in its proper setting.

AMBIGUOUS RHYTHM

How are we to understand the opening rhythm in the third movement of Brahms's Symphony No. 3 (Example 159)? The first two measures might be

EXAMPLE 159

superficially analyzed as consisting of two groups, an iamb and a trochee (see analysis in parentheses). But there is really only *one* impulse. As the cellists play the E-flat, we realize that the pressure of the impulse continues in tension and that we are not listening to a true end-accented rhythm. The whole impulse behaves like two feet fused into one group with the first accent as anacrusis to the second (Example 160*a*), or like a middle-accented rhythm in which two notes receive the single accent—a "distributed" accent (*b* in the example). The accompaniment, especially in the wood winds and violas, underlines the peculiar quality of the impulse.

The two chords in Example 161*a* accompany the two accents, or the one distributed accent, leaving the ambiguity unresolved; the viola figure emphasizes the primacy of the second accent (Example 160*a*) or the continuous pressure of the distributed accent (Example 160*b*), as one will. Both the feeling of fused rhythm and that of distributed accent have consequences in what follows.

EXAMPLE 160

EXAMPLE 161

EXAMPLE 162

After the first two feet (measures 1–4 of Example 159), the opening iamb (so to speak) appears separately (measures 5–8), although its security as an end-accented rhythm is gently undermined by the wood winds and violas, which give femine endings to the accompaniment (Example 161*b*).

This combination of circumstances gives us a strong sense that the peculiarity of the opening impulse is likely to be resolved finally by an end-accented rhythm. There would, for instance, be nothing technically impossible about the melody in Example 162. It would merely be poor; the feminine ending of the opening rhythm would have no consequences after its repetition in the second impulse; it would simply be replaced by masculine endings; the tension of the beginning would suffer a flabby letdown. Furthermore, there would be no real rhythm in measures 5–12 as a whole. There would be no temporal differentiation on the second architectonic level. Therefore, the four groups of measures 5–8 would not become a single group; neither would the four of measures 9–12. Measures 5–8 "want" to be an anacrusis to measures 9–12, but they have insufficient coherence to become one.

Here we can see again the intimate connection between rhythmic and melodic movements. The opening four measures are anacrustic for melodic reasons; they imply certain further linear movements, as in diagram *a* of Example 163. The upper movement (to G) is implied by the gap between F and A-flat and by the characteristic appoggiaturas; the lower, by tonality as well as by melodic direction. Furthermore, there is a rise in tension in the second foot. The double anacrusis, then, implies an accent of yet greater tension. This tension cannot come solely from an adequate morphological length and from consequential rhythmic activity (in spite of their importance); it must depend largely upon the

EXAMPLE 163

nature of the melodic line. And how does that line continue in our fictitious version?

In measures 5–8 (Example 163*b*) there are two gaps: E-flat–C, filled at the cadence, and F–D, left open; in measures 9–12, the F–D gap is filled by the E-flat appoggiatura, which leans on the weak penultimate D. This is unconvincing, because the E-flat is a non-essential note. Also, the tension of each of these four-measure groups is lower than that of the second foot in the melody: there, the B-flat–A-flat (measure 4) was strongly accented; here, it is a short upbeat.

In the actual melody (Example 159), measures 5–8 are almost exactly like the corresponding ones in the fictitious version. On the higher level, the rhythm is not yet completed. We have something like this: 1–2 3–4 5–6. But what

follows sets this right and thereby gains tremendously in tension.

In measure 7 we see the new process initiated. First, there is an anacrusis strongly emphasized by a turn about C. (Notice in this context the importance of the smoothed-out rhythm—♫ instead of ♪♪.) We are prepared for, though we do not necessarily expect, an afterbeat to the D in measure 8. But as the players move from each of the ensuing notes to the next (D–E-flat–E–F) the pressure continues, underlined by the accompaniment. The rhythm, which we every moment feel is about to have a feminine ending, continues to be masculine until, as we reach the high B-flat with its penetrating cello tone, we realize that the distributed accent, which was one of the feelings implicit in the opening rhythm, has here been stretched with a tension more than merely satisfying our expectation.

But the feminine ending is changing. It was secure in the opening two feet because of the stressed downbeat and the stationary harmony. The fact that the B-flat–A-flat–D of measure 4 was feminine in rhythm establishes a prior organization which allows us to feel here (in measure 9) that the same three notes have the same kind of rhythm. But the stress on the second beat of measure 9 and the change of harmony between this measure and the next prepare us to hear the three-note motive come to a masculine conclusion. That is, ♩. ♩ ♪ is prepared to change its feeling from trochaic to iambic. Indeed, this is what happens in the final measures of our excerpt. Notice the subtle pivoting here; it assists the change of rhythm. Notice also the beautiful clarity of melodic movement (occasioned chiefly by the lengthening of the notes B-flat and G in measures 9 and 10) and the way in which the two linear movements join as indicated in Example 164.

EXAMPLE 164

The ultimate G (in measure 12), which itself initiates a strongly anacrustic figure in the next measure, now makes in retrospect all that has been heard so far an anacrusis to the next twelve measures.

In this example, the opening rhythm has two implications (*a* and *b* in Example 160). Each of these has consequences in the ensuing development of the melodic line (measures 5–12). What happens in that development is clearly related to the opening rhythm, and it ends with a positive and unambiguous accent.

RHYTHMIC VAGUENESS

In the above Brahms excerpt, both rhythmic ambiguity and the ultimate removal of that ambiguity through development are part of the character of the music. Let us suppose, however, that the ambiguity of rhythm is such that to remove it would destroy the character of the music. In "Des pas sur la neige," from the first book of *Préludes* by Debussy, we find a piece with such an ambiguity.

As we think of the ostinato figure (Example 165), we are not sure of whether the essential melodic movement is D–E–F, with F as a resolution, or E–F–D, with F as an échappée. Analyses *a* and *b* are equally possible, for the treble melody in measures 2–4 supports both groupings (Example 166*a*). The heavy anacrusis in measure 2, which ends in no accent, leads us to hear the ostinato as ending on D (beginning of measure 3); the rhythm which is complete on the accented A of measure 4 leads us to hear it as ending on F. This accented A, to be sure, is not altogether satisfying as a goal of end-accented rhythmic motion, because it is at variance with the meter. The meter has been unequivocally estab-

EXAMPLE 165[1]

EXAMPLE 166

lished by the ostinato. Though the grouping of the ostinato is ambiguous, it is clear that the D receives the accent and that the F is unaccented. Therefore, when the melodic A in measure 4 is felt to be accented, it coincides with an unaccent in the ostinato.

Consider the effect of the unequivocal grouping of the ostinato which would result from rewriting the melody of measures 2–4 as in Example 166*b*. Now the E (measure 3) and the A (measure 4) are both accented, and they both fall on the metric downbeat established by the ostinato in the first two measures. The grouping of the ostinato becomes unambiguous; it is iambic, as in analysis *a* of Example 165. Also, the accented A in measure 4 coincides with the metric accent. But notice that the *character* of the music has been altered. It is still *expressif et*

[1] Permission to reprint granted by Durand et Cie, Paris, France, copyright owners; Elkan-Vogel Co., Inc., Philadelphia, Pa., agents.

douloureux, but it has lost its air of vague desolation. Now, it is precisely this air which is to arise from the piece as a whole. If the vagueness and ambiguity disappear, so will the character of the piece. One might well say that what is wanted here is clear vagueness and unambiguous ambiguity. The ostinato needs to be thought of and played without grouping, almost mechanically.

As we have seen, the accentless rhythm in measures 2–3 is followed by a rhythm which comes to a masculine ending in measure 4, but on a beat established by the ostinato as metrically weak. Put in another way, the heavy anacrusis of measure 2 seeks an accent on the downbeat of measure 3, but does not get it; thereupon, the even heavier anacrusis of measure 3 (and part of 4) gets its

EXAMPLE 167

EXAMPLE 168

accent, but not in the right place. In this manner, the rhythmic goal of the music is set up. But to reach that goal would be to destroy the character of the piece.

In order to retain this character, the rhythm has to be developed in such a way as to be end-accented but without satisfactory accent. We must be prevented from hearing feminine rhythms, and we must be made to hear anacruses everywhere.

For instance, out of context, measures 20–25 would probably group as in Example 167. There would be feminine endings on the primary rhythmic level. How does the composer set up a prior organization such that the accents in this passage sink to the subprimary level, and the rhythm on the primary level becomes completely anacrustic?

The answer lies in the treatment of measures 5–7 (Example 168*b*). We know from measures 2–4 what the goal of movement is. Now, in measures 5–7, we find built up the tense and long anacrusis out of which most of the rest of the piece grows. This is the crucial passage in the development of the piece, and the connection among rhythm, melody, and harmony is important to observe here.

As the melody moves up stepwise from A, it creates a series of dissonances with the harmony until it reaches D, whereupon, in relationship to the melodic movement from D to E in measures 2–3, it goes immediately to E and remains dissonant throughout measure 7. In this way, the melody is constantly on the move toward a goal; it is anacrustic. For a brief moment, on the D of measure 6, the goal appears to be attainable; the D anticipates it. But what is anticipated, an accented consonance, is not reached. The downward melodic motion of measure 7 indicates that the unsuccessful climb of measures 5–6 has to be attempted again, if the goal is to be reached.

Suppose the melody had been written as in *a* of the example. The tension would have been dissipated in a series of consonant afterbeats to the ostinato in measures 5–6, and the only dissonant note—the C in measure 6—would have resolved immediately onto the consonant D, which would then have become, melodically and harmonically, the goal of motion. An accent, instead of a renewal of an anacrusis, would have fallen on the first beat of measure 7 and the rest of the measure would have become almost an afterbeat. The accent would have been insecure (hence the "?" in the analysis), because of its tied-over anticipation, and such an insecurity would have been in character. But the serenity of the rising line of the preceding measures, and the lack of definition in those measures of an anacrustic feeling, would have been decidedly out of character. Once the anacrustic nature of measures 5–7 in the original piece has been established, the listener has the proper feeling for all the subsequent groupings, and the accentless rhythm can be maintained to the end.

We have been discussing a piece in which ambiguity of rhythm must be preserved. Let us turn to one in which failure to understand the grouping will create an ambiguity where there is none.

RHYTHMIC TRANSFORMATION

In the fourth piece of Schoenberg's *Sechs kleine Klavierstücke*, Op. 19 (Example 169), there is a striking difference in character between the beginning and the end. Clearly, much happens here in little space, unless one makes the mistake of assuming a merely whimsical juxtaposition of moods. The piece is very tight, not at all a fantasy or improvisation.

The opening impulse is a middle-accented rhythm with a two-unit anacrusis and an afterbeat bolstered by a shocking forte upbeat on the subprimary level (measure 2). This rhythm is marked "F.R." (for "fundamental rhythm") in the analysis.

The second impulse, because of prior organization, legato and staccato marks, and written meter, could be grouped as in Example 170. But the motivic organization, as indicated by the symbols *m* and *m'* in Example 169, will not support this grouping.

EXAMPLE 169[2]

[2] Permission granted by Universal Edition, Vienna, copyright owners; Associated Music Publishers, Inc., United States agent.

Now a false ambiguity could be created here by stressing this group in such a way as to make it conform with the first group and with the written meter. But the composer is careful in all his expression marks, and he indicates no stresses here; more important, if the piece is correctly heard mentally, the motivic structure will create groupings without any ambiguities. And only when that happens will the piece contain a chain of rhythmic development by transformation which connects the whole sequence of impulses in a particularly clear way.

The fundamental rhythm (F.R.) is that of the opening impulse in measures 1–2. Then comes the first transformation. Here, the reader will have noticed in the analysis (Example 169) that an overlapping occurs in the motivic structure of measure 3. The last note of *m'*, F, is at the same time the first note of *m* at the end of the measure. This means that a rhythmic shift is taking place. As one reaches the G on the second beat of the measure (an accented note on the subprimary level), it is the nucleus of the second unit in the fundamental rhythm's anacrusis.

EXAMPLE 170

When, however, one reaches the D in measure 3, *that* note becomes the nucleus of a *new* second unit in the anacrusis—a unit which, in effect, replaces its predecessor. As one starts moving through the group, then, the G (marked by *a* in measure 3) appears to be leading to the accent directly. As one goes farther, however, the D (marked by *b*) takes the place of the G in retrospect.

It will turn out that the eighth-note distance between *a* and *b* in measure 3 plays a part in the process of transformation. Indeed, at the end of this very impulse (in measure 4), the afterbeat is distant only by an eighth-note from its accent, instead of by a quarter-note, as it was in measure 2. This afterbeat is in the accompaniment and leaves the rhythm of the melody somewhat suspended.

In the next stage of development, the accompaniment (pianissimo), which is motivic, takes up the suggestion of eighth-note distance in a transformation of the motive of measure 3 (*m'*). As this transformation, which starts at the end of measure 5, moves into measure 6, the grace note (on the beat) provides an important link to subsequent developments.

At the same time, the main melody begins with the feminine rhythm of measure 2, but holds the afterbeat (F in measure 6) so long that it becomes an anacrusis and stretches the impulse, merging with the next stage, which begins in measure 6. The distance between *a* and *b* (measure 3) is important here, because this time the melody echoes the afterbeat, not on the next beat, but an eighth-note after it in measure 9 (Example 171). A feminine ending ♩♩ rather than the ♩ ♪ of measure 2 is now ready to enter the melody.

In the final transformation there is first an extremely intense and rapid review of the rhythmic and melodic essence of the first two impulses (measure 10). Here, because of prior organization, the rhythmic effect is complex. For instance, the distance from point *a* to point *b* in this measure is a sixteenth-note (cf. the small upbeat to measure 1), and that from *b* to *c* is the now familiar eighth; and the time-spaces between *d* and *e* and *e* and *f* are, in diminution, those of measure 3 (Example 172). All this serves as anacrusis to the last three measures, in which the afterbeat of the original rhythm (measure 2) has finally itself become a strong anacrusis, the whole being fused into the shape of the fundamental rhythm without the afterbeat (measures 11–13).

EXAMPLE 171

EXAMPLE 172

It was said above that the grace note in measure 6 formed an important link to subsequent developments. If we compare the rhythm of the F–F-sharp in measure 11 with the rhythm of the D–C–G in measure 6, we can see the connection between the motive *m'* and the powerful anacrusis of measures 11–12.

The lightness of the opening measures has turned into the grimness of the closing ones before our ears. In retrospect, we can understand the forte shock in measure 2. A process of rhythmic development can support not only a preservation of character, as in the Debussy Prelude, but also an utter transformation of character, as in this Schoenberg piece.

ANACRUSTIC DEVELOPMENT

Our final example will be the development section in the first movement of Beethoven's Symphony No. 8 (see pp. 195–202).

The exposition ends, we recall from the previous chapter, with four measures of anacrusis with no change of harmony (except for the addition of a B-flat) and no fundamental melodic motion. It is the end-accented rhythm on the primary level which measures here. This anacrusis leads to its accent as the repetition of the exposition begins.

Now, by means of repeating the exposition, the measuring rhythm of three eighth-notes followed by a quarter-note has acquired the specific meaning that the opening theme of the symphony will follow. The development section is, among other things, an exploitation of this meaning.

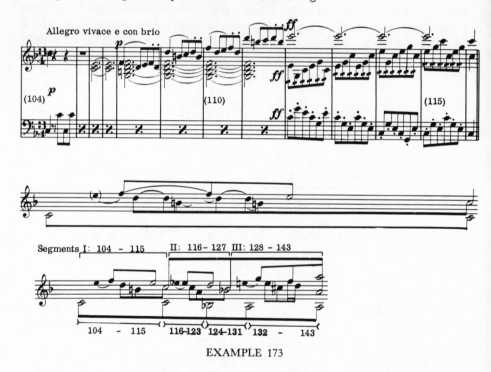

EXAMPLE 173

It begins by not moving. The weakness of the accent resulting from the failure to move is brought out by the absence of a sforzando on the first beat of measure 104, and the rhythm becomes forward-looking. In the ensuing passage (measures 104–43) the reduction of rhythm to meter—to measuring—puts the emphasis in the listener's mind on the larger rhythmic, melodic, and harmonic movements. Example 173 shows a diagram of this passage. There are three twelve-measure segments in it, the third of which is stretched by four more measures. Above the diagram is a reduction of the first segment, by an examination of which the reader can understand the method used in making the diagram.

This whole passage is an anacrusis. In the exposition, measures 96–99, followed by measures 100–103—tutti, fortissimo with sforzando, constituted an anacrusis to the return of the main theme (measures 1–12). Here, this sequence of events is delayed until the end of the passage, making the first two large segments of it incomplete in rhythm. Finally, the tutti, fortissimo with sforzando, in measures 140–43 refers forcefully to the meaning previously established for measures 100–103.

In each of the first two segments of the passage, the small melodic movements are closed out, throwing the attention on the segments as wholes. The A of the last segment then intensifies the feeling of impending movement.

The bass in Segment I is static. Indeed, it is a prolongation of the bass in measures 100–103, where it had already acquired the meaning of impending movement—a meaning made particularly forceful by the repetition of the exposition. It moves in Segment II when the linear direction of the whole passage can be seen—as soon, that is, as the F–E motion in the fundamental melody of Segment I is about to continue through E-flat to D. It moves in Segment III when the tonal tendency of the passage—the key of the eventual accent, D minor—can be clearly anticipated; the E introduced in measure 130 above the B-flat makes an A major triad the most likely continuation. But the accent thus extensively prepared becomes itself an anacrusis (Example 174).

The expected motive of measures 1–2, introduced with the stress of a syncopation in measure 143, is provided with afterbeats in the accompaniment. (Notice the sforzando in the violins in measure 144 and the wind chord in 145.) These make the rhythm ready to turn into an end-accented one with a strong anacrusis· The original pivoted rhythm of the motive now has a strongly stressed unaccent, and the last half of the foot has become middle-accented. The end of this foot is ready to become an inverted iamb, as it does, starting in measure 148, where the melodically detached C-sharp helps the next four notes to lead to the A of the following measure.

The melodic direction set up in measures 144–47 (A–B-flat) is continued by the C-sharp in 148, so that measures 148–51 begin as the accent to which the previous four measures are an anacrusis, but two factors turn this accent itself into an anacrusis: the measuring quality of the repeated foot, and the modulation to G minor. The whole passage, then, which began as the goal (accent) of measures 104–43, has itself taken on the quality of an anacrusis. This quality is now intensified by repetition in the following two passages, measures 152–59 and 160–67. Notice here the underlining of the upbeats by means of imitations, and the sense of beginning afresh at measures 152 and 160, only to find each time that the accent is part of a general anacrusis. At measure 168 there is no such fresh beginning. We are now in the final stage of this general anacrusis. Before discussing it, however, two more remarks on measures 144–67 may be helpful.

First, the 4 + 4 + 4 = 12 morphological lengths characteristic of the beginning of the development have given way to the more rapidly moving lengths, $2 + 2 + 4 = 8$. Second, the whole melodic and harmonic motion has been stepped up so that there is an increase in urgency here.

Now when we enter upon the final stage of the development section, yet another means of increasing the anacrustic quality is used: that of complete reduction to meter. The passage in measures 144–67 was incomplete in rhythm and was

EXAMPLE 174

neither a theme nor a series of themes, but its structured motion made it "theme-like." Now only undifferentiated repetition of motive within each morphological length is the method of development (Example 175), and the effect of such a method is like that of the last four measures in the exposition.

In this final passage, the morphological lengths are first reduced to four measures. Each length contains only one harmony. Notice the incomplete rhythms of the wind and timpani chords within the lengths. Each time the harmony changes,

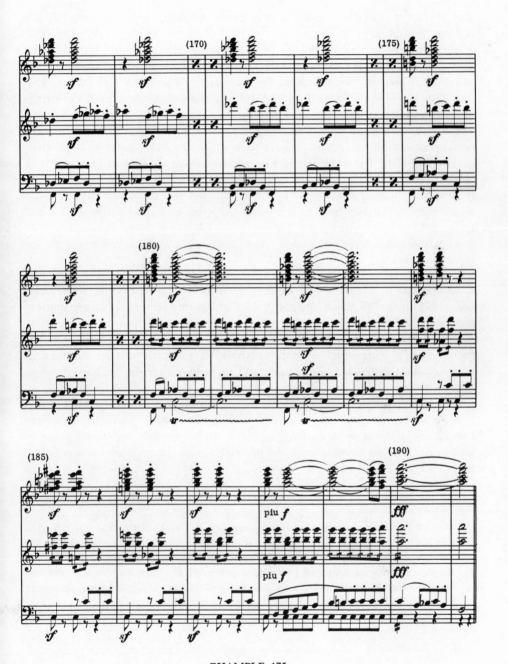

EXAMPLE 175

the rhythm is completed, only to emphasize the sense that the ending is but another beginning.

The next step in intensifying the anacrusis is the failure to move harmonically at measure 180. Added to this are the lengthened, loaded upbeat, the reduction of the morphological lengths from four measures to $2 + 2 = 4$ (finally to $1 + 1 + 1 + 1 = 4$ in measure 184), and the reduction of the rhythm in the strings almost to pulses (against the meter, as in measures 96–99). Then, in measures 184–87, the motive of measures 100–102 returns in the bass with all the force of its original meaning. Above it is a rhythm which, for all its apparent beginning-accented quality, has to be felt in the context as potentially end-accented with electric silences. It is at once complete and incomplete. The final intensification is furnished in measures 188–89 by the completed version of this rhythm, with its strongly stressed upbeat, and by the powerful anacrusis in the cellos and basses.

The whole development section, then, becomes a gigantic anacrusis to the recapitulation.

As movement of all kinds, especially melodic and harmonic movement, beginning on the lowest architectonic level, grows into larger and larger spans of time with cumulative effect, the shape of a piece—its tonal configuration in time—gradually emerges. And it is this shape, on all its levels of movement, which is the object of the art which we call "analysis." To practice this art, we need as many good implements as we can get, and we need to sharpen, perhaps reshape, them with use.

Rhythmic structure is, of course, only one aspect of this shape. But because it is a summarizing aspect, an understanding of rhythm—perhaps more than that of any of the other organizing forces of music—reveals in delicate detail as well as in dynamic development the full richness of the processes which create and mold musical experience.

EXERCISES

I. Make a rhythmic analysis of the recapitulation and coda of the first movement of Beethoven's Symphony No. 8. In what way does the fact that the recapitulation begins on a six-four chord affect the rhythm of the highest level?

II. Employing the concepts and procedures presented in this book, analyze the first movement of Mozart's Symphony No. 40 in G Minor. Write an essay discussing form, continuity, and rhythmic development in the whole movement.

EXTENDED EXAMPLES

EXAMPLE 176.—Chopin, Prelude in E-flat, Op. 24

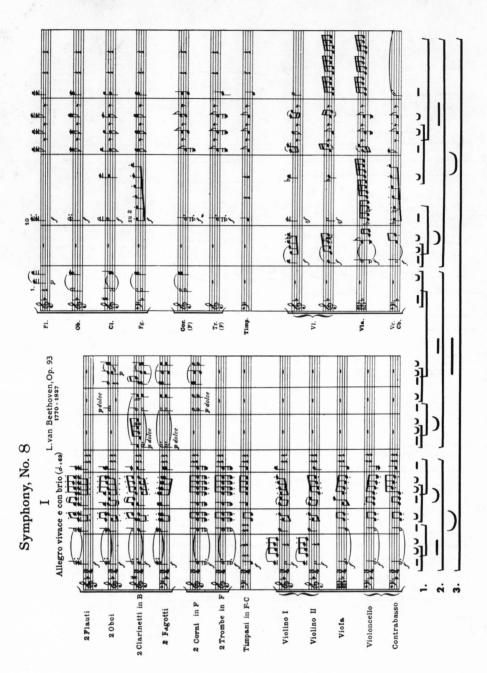

EXAMPLE 177.—Beethoven, Symphony No. 8

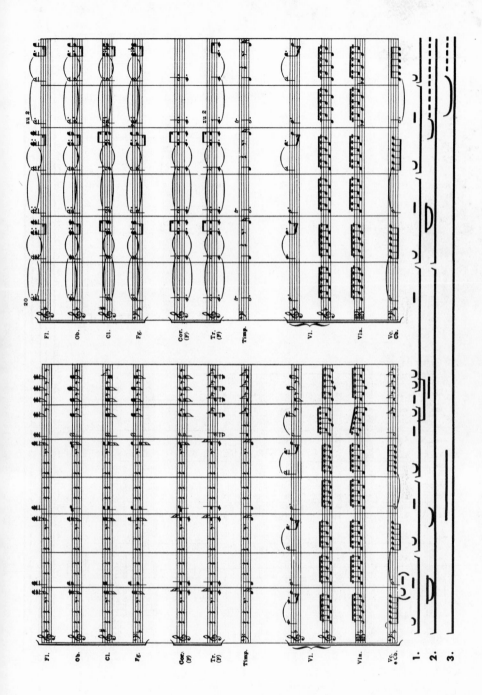

189

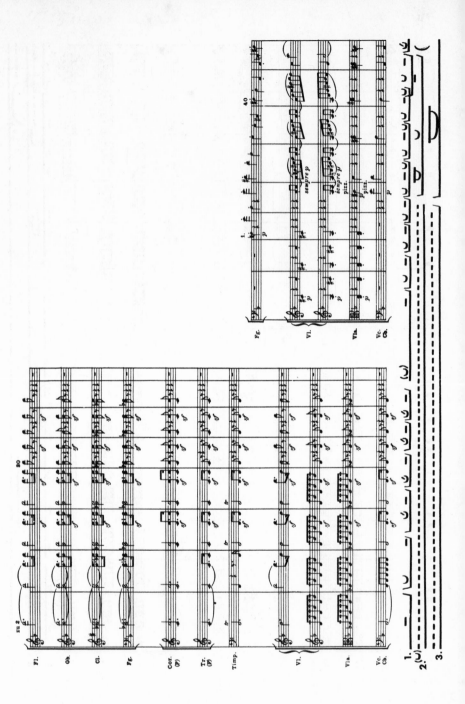

190

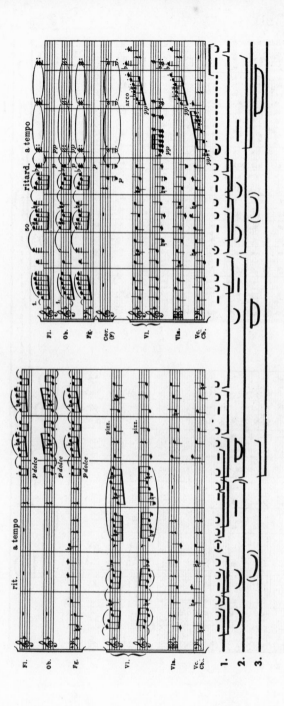

191

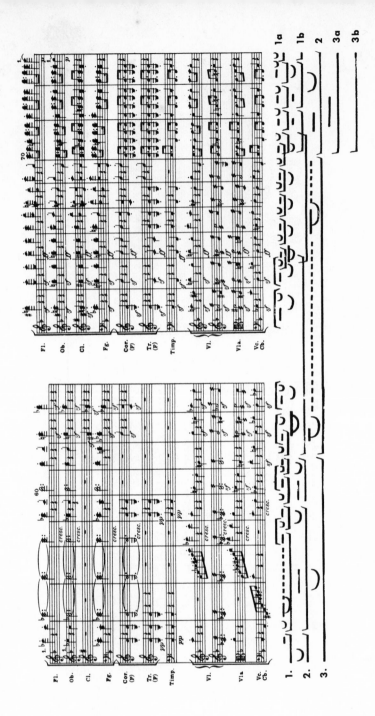

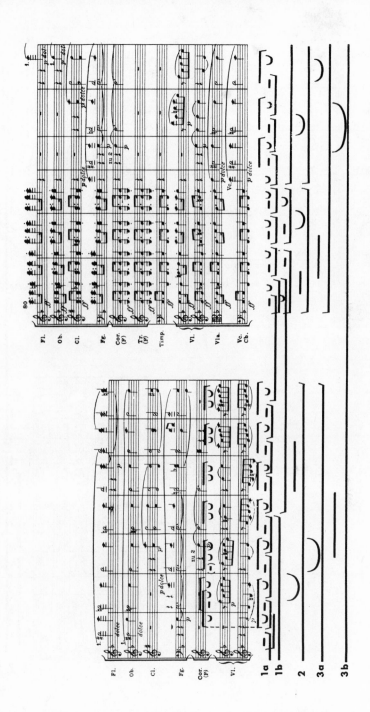

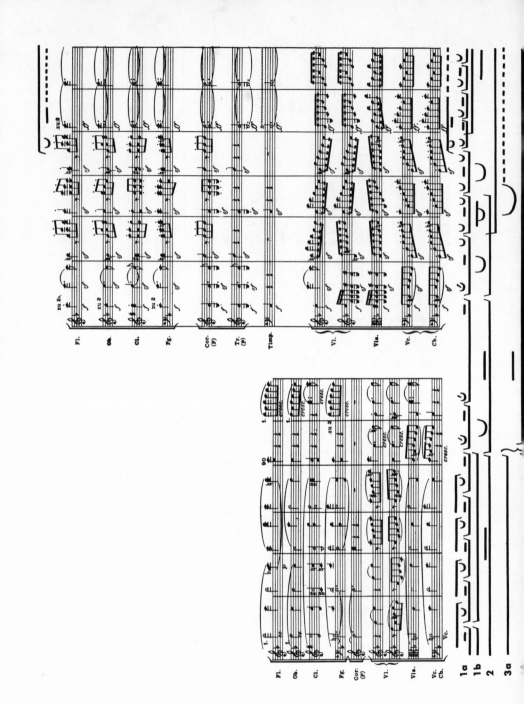

194

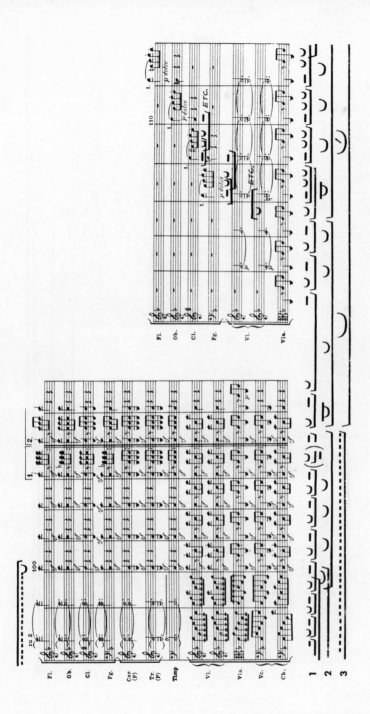

195

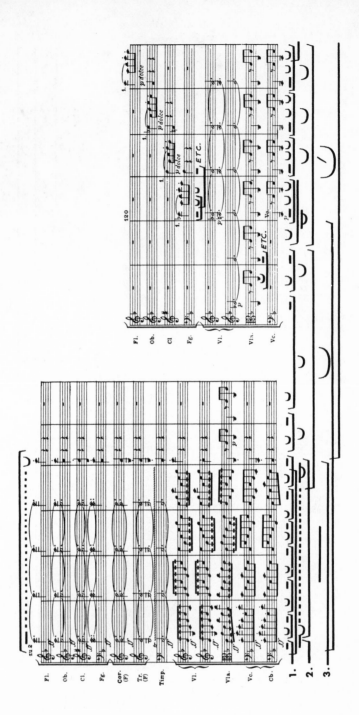

196

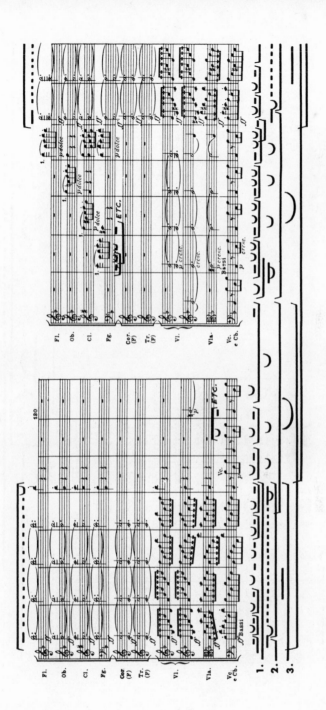

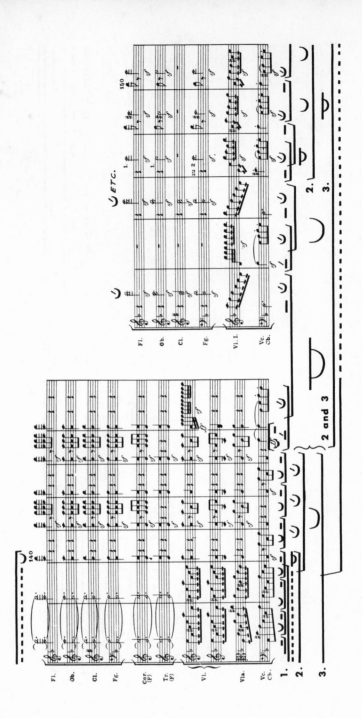

198

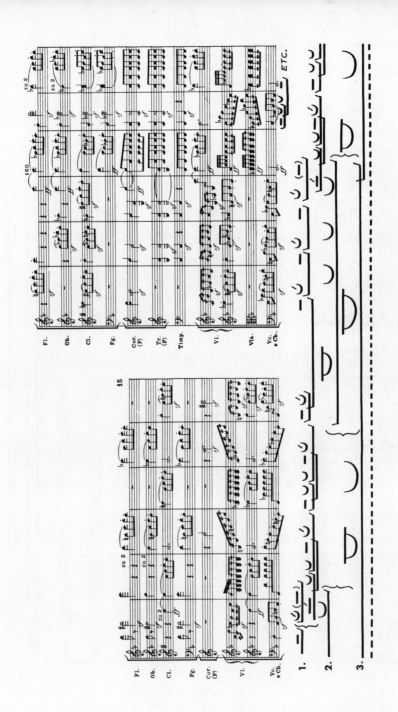

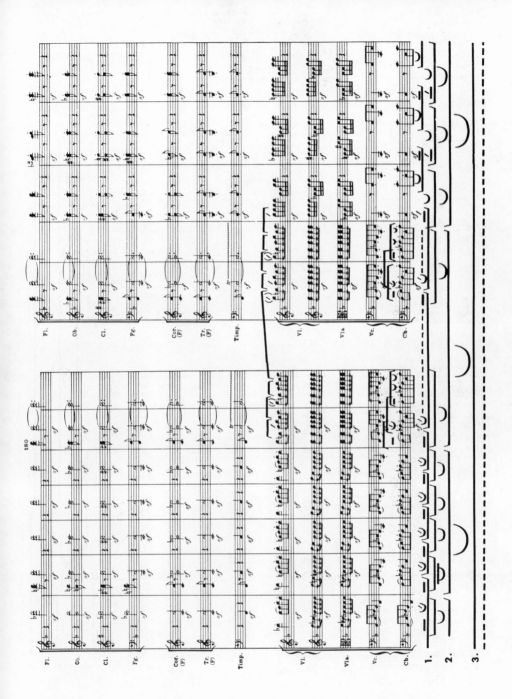

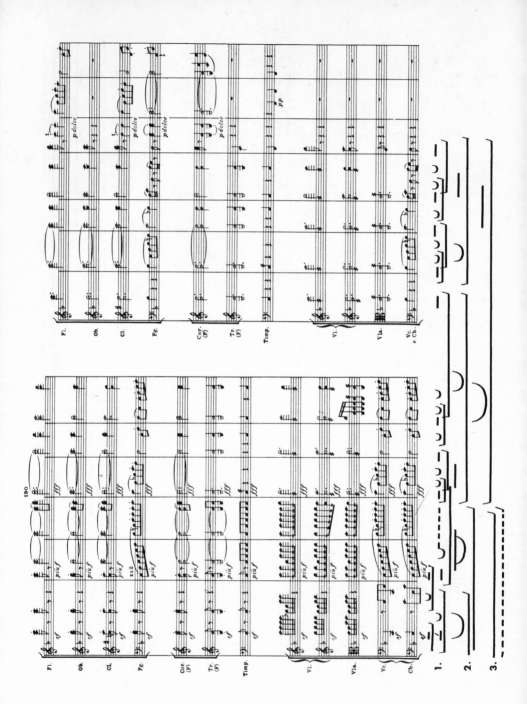

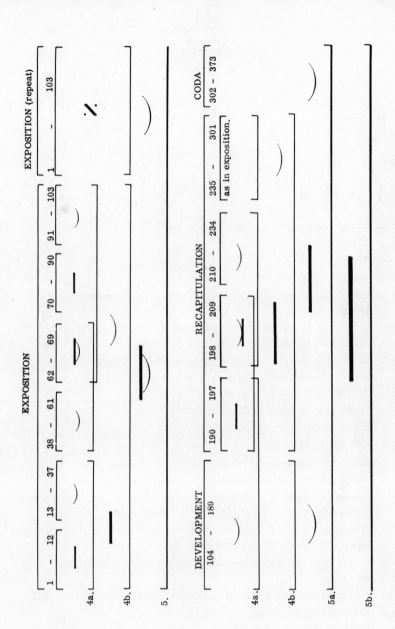

EXAMPLE 178.—Rhythmic analysis of the first movement of Beethoven's Symphony No. 8

LIST
OF
SYMBOLS

—   Accent

◡   Weak beat or group

(—)(◡)   Felt but unperformed beats or groups; or a parenthetical beat or group

▽   Beat or group at first presumed to be accented, but retrospectively understood to be weak

⌣̸   Beat or group at first presumed to be weak but retrospectively understood to be accented

⌒◡   Accent fused to a weak beat or group

◡⌒   Weak beat or group fused to an accent

◡⌒◡   Fused weak beats or groups

◡-------   Extended anacrusis

▽-------   Extended anacrusis at first presumed to be an accent

╱   Stress (stressed accent or group: ∠; stressed weak beat or group: ◡̸)

└─┘   Grouping, manifest or dominant; except where the analysis is above the example, when it indicates the latent grouping

┌─┐   Grouping, latent; except where the analysis is above the example, when it indicates the manifest grouping

└──   Grouping without a definite conclusion or which blends into another grouping

──┘   Grouping without a definite beginning point

└┴┘   Overlapping or pivoted rhythmic groups

└⌐┘   Splitting of one rhythmic level into two

INDEX

NOTE: The entry "Rhythm" interrelates the key terms used in this book.

Accent:
  defined, 7 f.
  further defined, 118 f., 125 ff. (see esp. 137)
  distributed, 168 ff.
Accented rest, 137 ff.
Accentuation, forced, 92 f.
Accompaniment:
  function of, 160 ff.
  influence of on rhythm, 17
Afterbeat, 125 ff. (see esp. 137)
Ambiguity, rhythmic (ambiguous grouping), 25, 32 ff., 54 ff., 168 ff.; *introduced*, 9
Amphibrach:
  introduced, 6
  on lower architectonic levels, 18 ff., 23 ff., 53 f., 54 (inverted)
  on higher architectonic levels, 80 ff.
  "attempted," 122
  "truncated," 135 f.
Anacrusis, 9, 73 f., 125 ff., 177 ff.:
  extended, 50 f., 129 ff.
  proximate vs. remote, 91
Analysis, rhythmic:
  as interpretation, 9
  and style, 57, 106 ff., 119 f.
  summarizing aspect of, 117, 123, 182
Analytical devices. *See* Reduction; Variation
Anapest:
  introduced, 6
  on lower architectonic levels, 18 ff., 23 ff., 51 f., 52 f., 32 (inverted)
  on higher architectonic levels, 68 ff.
Anticipation of future and evaluation of past, 62, 120
Architectonic levels:
  introduced, 2 f.
  relationship among, 120
Articulation and structure, 17 f.

Bar line, 88 f.
Beat placement, influence of on grouping, 15
Beginning-accented groups, 10. *See also* Dactyl; Trochee

Character of particular rhythms, 26 ff.
Closed groups, 39
Closed trochee, 30
Composite subgroups, 22 f.
Compound groups, 65
Consonance, metric, 108
Continuity:
  and rhythm, 144 ff. (see esp. 155)
  and form, 147 ff.
  and style, 161 ff.
  interrupted, 149

Dactyl:
  introduced, 6
  on lower architectonic levels, 18 ff., 23 ff., 43 ff., 45 ff., 31 (inverted)
  on higher architectonic levels, 75 ff.
Development:
  anacrustic, 177 ff.
  rhythmic, 168 ff.
Dissonance, metric, 108
"Distributed" accent, 168 ff.
Dominant organization (or rhythm), 13, 17 f.
Duration, influence of on rhythm, 10 f., 13 f., 24 ff., 29, 61. *See also* Temporal relationships
Dynamics:
  influence of on rhythm, 16
  interrelationship between and rhythm, 137
  "forced" vs. "natural," 127 ff.

Echo, *introduced*, 76
End-accented groups, 10. *See also* Anapest; Iamb
"Ex-theme," 158

Form:
  and continuity, 147 ff.
  and rhythm, 139, 144 ff. (see esp. 155)
Fused groups, 64 f.

Goldthwaite, W. S., 108 f.
Gombosi, O., 108 f.
Group inversion, 29 f.
Grouping, 1, 8 ff., 68 ff.

Harmony, influence of on rhythm, 14, 19 f., 39, 51 f., 61. *See also* Mobility
Hemiole, 4, 81, 88, 89

Iamb:
  introduced, 6
  on lower architectonic levels, 11 ff., 29 ff., 47 ff., 49 ff. (inverted)
  on higher architectonic levels, 70 ff.
Incomplete rhythm, 6, 79, 85, 139, 149 f., 157. *See also* Reduction to meter
Inferior rhythmic levels, 2
Instrumentation, influence of on rhythm, 16, 61. *See also* Style, and analysis
Interpretation and rhythm, 1
Inversion of grouping, 21, 32 (partial)
Inverted groups:
  amphibrach, 54
  anapest, 32
  dactyl, 31
  defined, 29
  iamb, 49 ff.
  trochee, 40
Latent organization (or rhythm), 13, 18
Links, 148
Lorenz, A., 146
Lower architectonic levels, 12 ff.

Melodic-rhythmic structure and syncopation, 102 ff.
Melody, influence of on rhythm, 14, 18 f., 24 ff., 29. *See also* Mobility
Meter:
  architectonic in nature, 2 f.
  defined, 4 f.
  and rhythm, 42, 96 f., 88 ff.
  latent, 89 ff.
  reduction to, 156 f.
  shifting and stable groups, 94 ff.
Metric:
  consonance, 108; dissonance, 108
  crossing, 81, 89, 106 ff.
Metric Equivalence, Principle of, 22 f.

Middle-accented groups, 10. *See also* Amphibrach
Mobility, 117 ff., 140 ff.
Morphological lengths, 144 ff.

Non-congruence of rhythm and meter, 89 ff., 164 ff.
"Non-theme" and continuity, 153 ff.

Open groups, 39
Ornamentation, influence of on rhythm, 21 f., 44, 49, 54
Overlapping, 148. *See also* Morphological lengths

Pace, 3 n. 1, 66
Partial inversion, 32
Performance and rhythmic structure, 8, 11, 15, 35, 164
Pivot, rhythmic, 23, 27, 62 ff.
Primary rhythmic level, 2
Prior organization, effect of on subsequent organization, 13, 33, 171
Pulse, 3 f.
Pyramidal groups, 65 ff.

Reduction, as analytical device, 69 f., 84 ff., 123
Reduction to meter, 156 f. *See also* Incomplete rhythm
Rest, accented, 137 ff.
Reversal, rhythmic, 77 f.
Rhythm:
  and other musical elements, 1
  as one of the temporal phenomena: pulse, meter, tempo, rhythm, 2 ff.
  defined as grouping, 6 f.
  elements of (*see* Accent; Afterbeat; Anacrusis; Echo)
  architectonic nature of:
    inferior levels, 2
    primary level, 2 (*see also* Composite subgroups; Compound groups; Metric Equivalence, Principle of)
    lower levels, 12 ff.
    higher levels, chaps. iii–vii (*see also* Fused groups; Non-congruence of rhythm and meter; Pivot; Pyramidal groups; Reversal)
  types of:
    beginning-accented (*see* Anapest; Iamb)
    middle-accented (*see* Amphibrach)
    end-accented (*see* Dactyl; Trochee)
    closed and open, 39
    ambiguous, 54 ff., 168 ff.
    vague, 171 ff.

incomplete, 79, 139, 149 f., 157 (*see also* Reduction to meter)
related to:
  anticipation of future and evaluation of past, 62, 120 (*see also* Dominant organization; Latent organization; Prior organization)
  beat placement, 15
  character, 34
  continuity, 144 ff.
  duration, temporal relationships, 13 f., 24 ff., 29, 61, 136, 147
  dynamics, 16, 137
  form, 139, 144 ff.
  harmony, 14, 19 f., 39, 51 f., 61
  instrumentation, 16, 61
  interpretation and performance, 1, 8, 11, 15, 35, 164
  melody, 14, 18 f., 24 ff., 29, 36 f.
  meter, 42, 96 f.
  mobility, 117 ff., 140 ff.
  morphological lengths, 144 ff.
  ornamentation, 21 f., 44, 49, 54
  stress, 8, 20 f., 24 ff., 29, 39
  suspension, 99 ff.
  syncopation, 31, 32, 99 ff., 102 ff.
  tension, 125 ff.
  texture (including accompaniment) 17, 160 ff.
  tie, 99 ff.
 development of, 168 ff.
 individuality of, 22
 summarizing aspect of, 117, 182
 transformation of, 174 ff.
Riemann, H., 147
Rubato, 8

Sachs, C., 108
Schenker, H., 70, 146
Stress:
 defined, 8

influence of on rhythm, 20 f., 24 ff., 29, 39
influence of on meter, 98 f.
and syncopation, 101 f.
Structural gap, 22, 91, 170
Style:
 and analysis, 106 ff., 119 f.
 and continuity, 161 ff.
Subprimary rhythmic levels, 2
Superior rhythmic levels, 2
Suspension, 99 ff.
Symbols, list of, 204
Syncopation, 31, 32:
 defined, 99 ff.
 and melodic-rhythmic structure, 102 ff.
 and stress, 101 f.

Tempo, 3; influence of on rhythm, 22 f.
Temporal relationships, influence of on rhythm, 61, 136, 147. *See also* Metric Equivalence, Principle of
Tension, 125 ff.
Texture and rhythm, 160 ff.
Theme:
 and continuity, 153 ff.
 incomplete, 153
Tie, 99 ff.
Transformation, rhythmic, 174 ff.
Trochee:
 introduced, 6
 on lower architectonic levels, 11 ff., 29 ff., 38 ff., 40 ff., 30 (closed), 40 f. (inverted)
 on higher architectonic levels, 74 f.

Upbeat. *See* Anacrusis

Vagueness, rhythmic, 171 ff.
Variation, as analytical device, 13 ff., 58, 116, 123 ff., 143, 167

INDEX
OF
MUSIC

Bach, J. S.:

Examples:

Brandenburg Concerto No. 5, i (Example 74), 55

Chamber Suite No. 1, 2d Bourrée (Example 73*a*), 54

English Suite No. 1 in A Major, 1st Bourrée (Example 85), 68

English Suite No. 3 in G Minor, Prelude (Example 68*a*), 51

French Suite No. 4 in E-flat Major, Sarabande (Example 51*a*), 40 f.

Mass in B Minor, "Laudamus Te" (Example 37*c, d, e*), 30 f.

Partita in D Minor for Unaccompanied Violin, Chaconne (Example 66*b*), 49 f.

Passion According to St. Matthew (Example 78), 62 f.

Six Little Preludes, 3d Prelude (Example 54), 42 f.

Twelve Little Preludes, 5th Prelude (Example 53*b*), 42

Well-tempered Clavier, Book II, Fugue in A Major (Example 155), 162 ff.

Well-tempered Clavier, Book II, Fugue in F-sharp Minor (Example 154), 162 ff.

References:

Brandenburg Concerto No. 1, iii, 51

Brandenburg Concerto No. 2, i, 64

Brandenburg Concerto No. 3, i, 48

Brandenburg Concerto No. 4, ii, 52

English Suite No. 4, Sarabande, 43

French Suite No. 2 in C Minor, Gigue, 48

French Suite No. 5 in G Major, Bourrée, 68; Gavotte, 64, 70; Gigue, 75

Fugues, 161 f.

Orchestra Suite No. 2 in B Minor, i, 54; Rondeau, 53

Orchestra Suite No. 3 in D Major, iv, 47; Gavotte, 53

Orchestra Suite No. 4 in D Major, 1st Bourrée, 54

Sonata in C Minor for Unaccompanied Cello, Sarabande, 43

Sonata No. 6 for Violin and Clavier, iii, 45

Toccata in G Minor for Clavier, 74

Well-tempered Clavier, Book I, Prelude XII, 54; XX, 45

Exercises:

Chamber Suite No. 4 in D Major, iii, 115

Prelude and Fugue in A Major for Organ, Fugue, 115

Well-tempered Clavier, Book II, A-Minor Fugue, 167

Well-tempered Clavier, Book II, G-Minor Fugue, 167

Bartók, B.:

Example:

Piano Concerto No. 3, iii (Examples 120–22), 106–8

References:

Sonata for two Pianos and Percussion, i, 48

String Quartet No. 3, 89

Exercises:

Piano Sonata (1926), i, 116

Violin Concerto, i, 116

Beethoven, L. van:

Examples:

Bagatelle Op. 119, No. 10 (Example 48), 39

Concerto in B-flat for Piano, iii (Example 37*a, b*), 30

Grosse Fuge (Examples 156–58), 164–66
Overture to Egmont, Allegro (Example 52*a*), 41
String Quartet Op. 130, Alla danza tedesca (Example 57), 44
String Quartet Op. 131, iv (Example 70*b*) 52 f.
Symphony No. 2 in D Major, Scherzo (Example 59), 45
Symphony No. 3 in E-flat Major, i (Examples 137–39), 137 ff.; Scherzo (Examples 88–89), 71 ff.
Symphony No. 4 in B-flat Major, Scherzo (Example 106), 92 f.
Symphony No. 5 in C Minor, iv (Example 64), 48 f.
Symphony No. 8 in F Major, i (Examples 148–52, 173–75, 177–78), 153 ff., 177 ff.; ii (Example 110), 97 f.
Symphony No. 9 in D Minor, Scherzo (Examples 93–95), 77 ff.

References:
"Archduke" Trio (Op. 97), Scherzo, 42
Concerto in D Major for Violin, iii, 68
Leonore Overture No. 3, 47
Piano Trio Op. 1 No. 3, iii, 54; iv, 40
Piano Trio Op. 97 ("Archduke"), iii, 80
Serenade Op. 25, vi, 40
String Quartet Op. 18 No. 3, ii, 49; iii, 54
String Quartet Op. 18 No. 4, i, 47; ii, 51, 52
String Quartet Op. 95, iii, 45
String Quartet Op. 127, iii, 70, 80
String Quartet Op. 130, i, 57; ii, 64
String Trio Op. 9 No. 1, i, 65
Symphony No. 1 in C Major, ii, 51, 54
Symphony No. 3 in E-flat Major, i, 57; Scherzo, 83, 93
Symphony No. 5 in C Minor, i, 48, 153; iv, 93
Symphony No. 7 in A Major, i, 150; iii, 43
Symphony No. 9 in D Minor, i, 49; Scherzo, 5

Exercises:
Bagatelle Op. 119 No. 1, 116, 167
Piano Sonata Op. 111, i, 116
Symphony No. 3 in E-flat Major, i, 143
Symphony No. 8 in F Major, i, 182

Berlioz, H.:
Example:
Symphonie fantastique, iii (Example 66*a*), 49
Reference:
Symphonie fantastique, ii, 73 f.

Binchois, G.:
Exercise:
"De plus en plus," 116

Borodin, A.:

Example:
String Quartet in D Major, ii (Example 90), 74 f.

Brahms, J.:
Examples:
Concerto in D Major for Violin, ii (Example 60*a*), 46
Sonata in A Major for Violin and Piano, ii (Example 51*c*), 40 f.
String Quartet in A Minor, Finale (Examples 96–97), 81 ff.
Symphony No. 3 in F Major, iii (Examples 159–64), 168 ff.
Symphony No. 4 in E Minor, iii (Example 112), 99 f.
Variations on a Theme by Haydn Op. 56a, 6th Variation (Example 49), 39
References:
Horn Trio, i, 53
Intermezzo Op. 76 No. 3, 83
Piano Trio Op. 101, i, 52
Rhapsody Op. 119 No. 4, 40
String Quartet in A Minor, iii, 80
String Quintet Op. 88, ii, 51
Symphony No. 1 in C Minor, iii, 64; iv, 49
Symphony No. 2 in D Major, iii, 45, 51
Symphony No. 4 in E Minor, i, 48
Variations on a Theme by Handel, i, 40; ii, iii, vi, 57
Variations on a Theme by Paganini, iii, 54
Exercises:
Intermezzo Op. 116 No. 6, 143
Sonata in D Minor for Violin and Piano, i, 116
String Quartet in A Minor, i, 116

Bruckner, A.:
Example:
Symphony No. 9, i (Examples 107–9), 94 ff.
Exercise:
Symphony No. 7, i, 142

Chopin, F.:
Examples:
Etude Op. 10 No. 9 (Examples 134–35), 127 ff.
Mazurka Op. 41 No. 3, 43
Mazurka Op. 50 No. 2 (Example 72*b*), 53 f.
Mazurka Op. 56 No. 1 (Example 56*b*), 43 f.
Nocturne Op. 48 No. 1 (Example 67*a*), 50
Prelude Op. 24 No. 1 (Example 46), 36 f.
Prelude Op. 24 No. 4 (Example 46), 36 f.
Prelude in E-flat Op. 24 No. 19 (Examples 132–33, 176), 125 ff., 151 ff.
References:
Etude Op. 10 No. 11, 51

Chopin, F.—*Continued*
  References—*Continued*
    Etude Op. 25 No. 5, 40
    Fantasie-Impromptu Op. 66, 70
    Mazurka Op. 50 No. 3, 45
    Nocturne Op. 9 No. 2, 75
    Nocturne Op. 15 No. 3, 48
    Nocturne Op. 37 No. 1, 40
    Polonaise Op. 40 No. 1, 83
    Polonaise Op. 71 No. 1, 40, 49
    Valse Brillante Op. 34 No. 3, 74
    Waltz Op. 18, 45
    Waltz Op. 64 No. 1, 43
    Waltzes, 73
  Exercises:
    Etude Op. 10 No. 10, 116
    Etude Op. 25 No. 8, 116
    Prelude Op. 28 No. 1, 87

Debussy, C.:
  Examples:
    Nocturnes for Orchestra, "Nuages" (Example 77), 57
    Préludes, Book I, "Des pas sur la neige" (Examples 165–68), 171 ff.
  Reference:
    Nocturnes for Orchestra, "Fêtes," 48
Dufay, G.:
  Example:
    Missa Sancti Jacobi, Kyrie (Examples 123–25), 109 ff.
Dvořák, A.:
  References:
    String Quartet Op. 51, iv, 80
    String Quartet Op. 96, i, 68
    Symphony No. 5 in E Minor, iv, 74

Fauré, G.:
  Reference:
    Piano Quartet Op. 15, i, 48
Folksongs:
  "Ach du Lieber Augustin" (Examples 25–28, 30, 34–36, 38–41, 44), 24–26, 29–32, 34
  "Alouette," 150
  "Au clair de la lune" (Examples 142–47), 144–51; Exercise, 167
  "Suse, liebe Suse" (Examples 42, 43, 45), 33 ff.
  "Twelve Days of Christmas, The," 150
  "Twinkle, Twinkle, Little Star" (Examples 2–24, 33), 9, 12–23, 28
Franck, C.:
  Example:
    Piano Quintet in F Minor, i (Example 61), 46 f.

Reference:
  Symphony in D Minor, i, 47
Gedalge, A.:
  Exercise:
    Fugue subject, 167

Handel, G. F.:
  Examples:
    Concerto Grosso No. 1, iv (Example 76), 56 f.
    Concerto Grosso No. 2, iii, 43
    Concerto Grosso No. 3, Polonaise (Example 68b), 51
    Concerto Grosso No. 8, iii (Example 50a), 39 f.
    Messiah, "Ev'ry Valley" (Examples 113–14), 100–102
  References:
    Concerto Grosso No. 1, iii, 52
    Concerto Grosso No. 4, iii, 48
    Concerto Grosso No. 5, v, 40
    Concerto Grosso No. 6, v, 45; Musette, 52
    Concerto Grosso No. 7, i, 65; iii, 70
    Concerto Grosso No. 9, ii, 75; Gigue, 68
  Exercise:
    Concerto Grosso No. 7, v, 116
Haydn, F. J.:
  Examples:
    Piano Sonata No. 37 in D Major, i (Example 63), 48
    String Quartet Op. 33 No. 3, iv (Example 47), 38
    String Quartet Op. 54 No. 3, iii (Example 50b), 40
    Symphony No. 92 in G Major ("Oxford"), Finale (Examples 31–33), 27 f.
    Symphony No. 94 in G Major ("Surprise") iv (Examples 81–84), 65 ff.
    Symphony No. 97 in C Major ("Salomon"), Minuet (Examples 98–101), 83 ff.; Finale (Example 71), 53
    Symphony No. 100 in G Major ("Military"), Finale (Example 92), 76 f.
    Symphony No. 102 in B-flat Major, Minuet (Example 72a), 53
    Symphony No. 104 in D Major ("London"), iii (Examples 29, 140–41), 26, 140 ff.; iv (Example 60b), 46
  References:
    Piano Sonata No. 33 in C Major, i, 49
    Piano Sonata No. 35 in D Major, Finale, 54
    String Quartet Op. 20 No. 5, iii, 75
    String Quartet Op. 55 No. 3, i, 43
    String Quartet Op. 71 No. 1, i, 53; iv, 49, 54
    String Quartet Op. 74 No. 3, i, 51
    String Quartet Op. 76 No. 5, iv, 70

Symphony No. 45 in F-sharp Minor ("Farewell"), Finale, 120
Symphony No. 94 in G Major ("Surprise"), ii, 40; iii, 64
Symphony No. 97 in C Major ("Salomon"), Minuet, 71; iv, 57
Symphony No. 101 in D Major ("The Clock"), i, 74
Symphony No. 104 in D Major ("London"), i, 51
Exercises:
String Quartet Op. 77 No. 2, ii, 116
Symphony No. 97 in C Major ("Salomon"), Minuet, 87
Symphony No. 104 in D Major ("London"), iii, 116
Humperdinck, E.:
Reference:
Hänsel und Gretel, 36

Mendelssohn, F.:
Example:
Symphony No. 4 in A Major ("Italian"), i (Example 80), 64
Mozart, W. A.:
Examples:
Eine kleine Nachtmusik (K. 525), iv (Example 65), 49
Horn Quintet (K. 407), ii (Example 52b), 41 f.
Serenade for Winds (K. 361), i (Example 67b), 50
String Quartet in G Major (K. 387), Minuet (Example 51b), 40 f.
String Quartet in C Major (K. 465), iv (Example 75), 55 ff.
String Quintet in C Minor (K. 406), i (Example 91), 76
Symphony No. 21 in A Major (K. 134), Minuet (Example 69), 51 f.
Symphony No. 40 in G Minor (K. 550), Minuet (Examples 116, 118, 119), 102 ff.
Symphony No. 41 in C Major (K. 551) ("Jupiter"), i (Examples 127–31), 120 ff.; ii (Examples 102–5), 89 ff.; Finale (Example 126), 117 ff.
References:
Clarinet Quintet (K. 541), iv, 40
Concerto in D Minor for Piano and Orchestra (K. 466), ii, 3 n. 1
Divertimento in D Major (K. 205), ii (trio), 43
Divertimento in B-flat Major (K. 270), iv, 54
Divertimento in B-flat Major (K. 287), v, 80

Piano Quintet in E-flat Major (K. 452), iii, 75
Quintet in G Minor (K. 516), Trio, 145
Serenade in D Major (K. 239), i, 47; iii, 54
String Quartet in G Major (K. 387), iii, 48
String Quartet in D Minor (K. 421), iii, 40; iv, 68
String Quartet in C Major (K. 465), iii, 65
String Quartet in D Major (K. 499), iv, 80
String Quartet in D Major (K. 575), iii, 43
Symphony No. 27 in G Major (K. 199), iv, 52
Symphony No. 33 in B-flat Major (K. 319), i, 52; iv, 49
Symphony No. 35 in D Major (K. 385), iv, 74
Symphony No. 38 in D Major (K. 504), ii, 83
Symphony No. 39 in E-flat Major (K. 543), i, 52; iii, 45
Symphony No. 40 in G Minor (K. 550), i, 153 f.
Symphony No. 41 in C Major (K. 551) ("Jupiter"), iii, 51
Exercises:
Sonata in A Major for Violin and Piano (K. 305), i, 116
Symphony No. 40 in G Minor (K. 550), i, 182
Symphony No. 41 in C Major (K. 551) ("Jupiter"), i, 142; ii, 57; Minuet, 87
Variations on "Ah, vous dirai-je, maman" (K. 265), 58

Purcell, H.:
Example:
Sonata for Two Violins and Continuo ("Golden"), i (Example 55), 43

Ravel, M.:
Reference:
Le tombeau de Couperin, i, 75
Rimski-Korsakov, N.:
Example:
Schéhérazade, iii (Example 153), 160 f.

Schoenberg, A.:
Example:
Sechs kleine Klavierstücke Op. 19, iv (Examples 169–72), 174 ff.
Reference:
String Quartet No. 3, iv, 70
Schubert, F.:
Examples:
Piano Trio in B-flat Major, i (Example 87), 70 f.

Schubert, F.—*Continued*
Examples—*Continued*
String Quartet in A Minor, iv (Example 79), 63 f.
String Quartet in G Major, i (Example 73*b*), 54
String Quartet "Death and the Maiden," ii (Example 70*a*), 52
Symphony No. 5 in B-flat, Minuet (Example 117), 103 f.
Wanderer-Fantasie, Presto (Example 53*a*), 41 f.
References, 5:
Impromptu Op. 142 No. 4, 45
Moments Musicaux Op. 94, v, 40
Piano Quintet Op. 114, iii, 70
Piano Trio Op. 99, i, 65
Songs, 73
String Quartet in D Minor, i, 64
String Quartet Op. 29, ii, 40
Symphony No. 8 in B Minor, i, 51
Wanderer-Fantasie, Allegro, 47
Exercises:
Impromptu Op. 142 No. 4, 116
Symphony No. 7 in C Major, i, 142
Schumann, R.:
Examples:
Carnaval, "Davidsbündler" March (Example 56*a*), 43 f.
Fantasiestücke, "Des Abends" (Example 58*b*), 44 f.
Papillons, No. 6 (Example 86), 69 f.
String Quartet Op. 41 No. 1, i (Example 62), 47
Symphonic Etudes, No. 9 (Example 58*a*), 44
Symphony No. 4 in D Minor, Scherzo (Example 115), 102

References:
Carnaval, "Valse Allemande," 40
Davidsbündler, ii, 65
Fantasiestucke, "Grillen," 52; "Ende vom Lied," 54
Kinderszenen, iv, 75
Piano Concerto in A Minor, iii, 88 f.
String Quartet Op. 41 No. 1, ii, 74
Symphonic Etudes, No. 5, 43; No. 10, 48
Symphony No. 4 in D Minor, ii, 68
Exercises:
Fantasiestücke, "Grillen," 143
Fantasiestücke, "Warum," 167
String Quartet Op. 44 No. 1, ii, 116
Symphony No. 1 in B-flat Major, iii, 116
Stravinsky, I.:
Example:
The Rite of Spring, "Dance of the Adolescents" (Example 111), 98 f.
Reference:
Suite No. 2 for Small Orchestra, iv, 80
Exercise:
Suite No. 2 for Small Orchestra, ii, 116

Tchaikovsky, P. I.:
Reference:
Symphony No. 5 in E Minor, ii, 64
Exercise:
Symphony No. 6 in B Minor, i, 143

Wagner, R:
Example:
Tristan und Isolde, Act II, Introduction (Example 136), 129 ff., 139, 142
Reference:
Tristan und Isolde, Act III, Scene 2, 4
Exercise:
Tristan und Isolde, Act II, Introduction, 143